Lost Restaurants

of

BALTIMORE

Lost Restaurants

of

BALTIMORE

SUZANNE LOUDERMILK AND KIT WASKOM POLLARD

AMERICAN PALATE

Published by American Palate

A Division of The History Press

Charleston, SC

www.historypress.com

Copyright © 2019 by Suzanne Loudermilk and Kit Waskom Pollard

All rights reserved

First published 2019

Manufactured in the United States

ISBN 9781467140669

Library of Congress Control Number: 2019945077

To our husbands, who gave us support when we needed it most.

Contents

Acknowledgements...11

Introduction..13

1. Thompson's Sea Girt House
   Crab Cakes and More, 1885–1991...15

2. Connolly's Seafood House
   A Harbor Fish House, 1886–1991...19

3. Horn & Horn
   A Place for Everyone, 1891–1977..24

4. Women's Industrial Exchange
   Tomato Aspic and Deviled Eggs, Early 1900s–2014..............................28

5. Miller Bros.
   A Favorite Meeting Place, 1912–1980s...34

6. Hutzler's Colonial Tea Room
   Refined Department Store Dining, 1917–1984...................................39

7. The Southern Hotel
   A Posh Dining Room, 1918–1964...43

CONTENTS

8. Martick's Restaurant Francais
   Bohemian Vibe with a Doorbell, 1920s–2008 47

9. Maison Marconi
   Old-Fashioned and Traditional, 1920–2005 52

10. Haussner's
    A Sprawling Masterpiece, 1926–1999 57

11. Chesapeake Restaurant
    An Illustrious Institution, 1933–1986 61

12. Burke's Restaurant
    Known for Power Lunches, 1934–2010 66

13. Read's Drug Store
    A Lunch Counter Sit-In, 1934–1970s 69

14. Peerce's Plantation
    Genteel Setting in the Country, 1937–2001 74

15. Velleggia's
    One of the Oldest Italian Restaurants, 1937–2008 80

16. Obrycki's Crab House
    Bibs, Mallets and Spicy Seasoning, 1944–2011 85

17. The Eager House
    Expense Accounts and Celebrations,
    1947–1986 and 1993–1998 88

18. Jimmy Wu's New China Inn
    Chinese Food to Savor, 1948–1983 92

19. Harvey House
    Named After an Invisible Rabbit, 1951–1993 96

20. Pimlico Hotel
    Where the Famous Would Go, 1951–1991 99

21. Danny's
     Upscale and French, 1961–1991 104

22. Bernie Lee's Penn Hotel
     A Social and Political Club, 1967–1974 108

23. The Golden Arm
     Where the Colts Came to Dine, 1968–1995 112

24. The Crease
     An Original Fern Bar, 1972–2016 116

25. Brass Elephant
     An Elegant, Historic Setting, 1977–2009 119

26. Hersh's Orchard Inn
     Special Occasion Dining in the 'Burbs, 1979–1997 123

27. Gampy's
     Introducing an Eclectic Menu, 1979–1995 128

28. Harvey's at Green Spring Station
     A Hot Spot in Baltimore County, 1979–2000 132

29. Louie's Bookstore Café
     Food with an Artistic Twist, 1981–2001 137

30. Jeannier's
     A Classic French Restaurant, 1986–2005 145

31. Polo Grill
     A Clubby Classic, 1990–2002 149

32. Spike & Charlie's
     Elevating the Culinary Scene, 1991–2004 153

33. Wild Mushroom
     A Focus on Fungi, 1995–2000 158

Contents

34. Della Notte Ristorante
    A Little Italy Gem, 1997–2013...164

35. The Chameleon
    A Locavore Pioneer, 2001–2012.......................................168

Index..173
About the Authors...176

Acknowledgements

We are grateful to Brian Boston; Micah Connor of the Maryland Historical Society; Jim Considine; Amy Davis; Rick K. Davis and Joyce V. Garczynski of Towson University; John DeFerrari; Paul Esbrandt; Patrick Ford; Peggy Fox; Charlie Gjerde; Spike Gjerde; Jenny Hope; Brennen Jensen; Elizabeth Large; John McGrain; Patty Novik; Francis O'Neill of the Maryland Historical Society; Thea Osato; Jennifer Price; Jan Purnell; Steve Rivelis; Dan Rodricks; Jimmy Rouse; Karene Connolly-Smith; Rick Stielper of Carroll Architectural Shade; Anne Tallent; Justin Williams of the Baltimore Museum of Industry; Yuri Zietz of the Baltimore County Library; and William Zvarick. We also want to thank our families and everyone who had to listen to us talk about our work in progress.

Introduction

The story of *Lost Restaurants of Baltimore*—beloved restaurants that have closed—is more than just a tale of eating establishments that have come and gone; it is a heartfelt story about the ever-changing landscape of Baltimore and the people who live there.

In this book, we will explore the stories behind thirty-five restaurants, from those that reigned supreme in the late 1880s to those whose impact in the 1990s and early twenty-first century influence our dining culture today. We will also include some stalwarts from Baltimore County. We know there are many more restaurants that deserve recognition, but unfortunately, space constraints limited our selection.

The world has changed a lot since the first restaurants in our book opened. Some of the earliest places were products of segregation, when inclusivity wasn't understood. The physical landscape shifted, too; construction projects—like Harborplace and Harbor East—offered new choices for dining, traffic patterns were rearranged, city dwellers decamped for the suburbs, and, just a generation later, they headed back to the city. Some restaurants were able to capitalize on the changes, while others weren't so lucky. Some restaurants' locations became inconvenient for customers, and some suffered when their cuisines were not popular anymore as diners' tastes evolved. Some traditional dishes—think terrapin soup and heavy German fare—fell by the wayside as Americans expanded their palates. Huge menus with multiple pages gave way to shorter, more creative lists featuring seasonal and local ingredients.

Despite all of this, Baltimoreans are a nostalgic group of people who continue to celebrate the quirkiness of Charm City's inhabitants. Locals always love a character: from the industrious and glad-handing Jimmy Wu to the dyspeptic charms of Morris Martick and namesake hosts like Bernie Lee and Hersh Pachino. Whether restaurants in Baltimore were driven by a single, sparkling leader or thrived because of a synchronized crew of many, they all influence today's restaurateurs, who are building establishments on the strengths and hard-learned lessons of those who came before.

Sometimes, a current restaurant's homage to the past is more overt. One of the best-selling dishes on Chef Brian Boston's menu at the Milton Inn in Sparks, Maryland, is the filet Chesapeake. This was a dish found in several midcentury menus, including that of Peerce's Plantation, where Chef Boston got his start. Mama's on the Half Shell in Canton pays tribute to Connolly's Seafood House with a list of the defunct restaurant's specialties on its menu. Though times change, Baltimore diners are always on the hunt for a restaurant that feels like home. And if there's a top-notch crab cake on the menu, that's even better!

While writing this book, we enjoyed talking to people about the restaurants they frequented that they now miss. During these conversations, we discovered that Jimmy Rouse learned the restaurant business while working as a waiter at Martick's. He then went on to successfully run Louie's Bookstore Café, which, in turn, inspired Spike Gjerde to open the bookstore café, Bird in Hand, in Charles Village. Others, like Rob Cernak, absorbed the nuances of the trade from their families. Cernak started working at an early age with his parents, Richard and Rose, at Obrycki's. His son, Rob Jr., is now general manager of the family's airport eateries. Their recollections about waiters and waitresses, the decor and the dishes they savored were thoughtful and comforting. Through their stories, we were reminded of all we love about Baltimore, its citizens and its food.

To pay respect to future chefs, we are donating a portion of our royalties to Maryland ProStart, a high school program that trains the restaurateurs of tomorrow. We can't wait to find out what their stories will be.

1

Thompson's Sea Girt House

CRAB CAKES AND MORE
1885–1991

When Thompson's Sea Girt House opened on Newkirk Street in Canton in 1885, Baltimore was a different place. Horses pulled carriages along the streets, the waterfront had not yet been fully industrialized and central air conditioning was decades away from widespread availability. But even then, seafood reigned supreme in Baltimore. And Thompson's was the place to get it.

Thompson's was named for its founder, George Thompson, and its location; *girt* means "surrounded by the sea." The restaurant was originally located near a 450-foot pier that jutted into the Patapsco River. During the early twentieth century, the original building was replaced with a pavilion that looked out over the river. In 1949, the restaurant moved north, to a Govans location at the corner of York Road and Belvedere Avenue, where it remained until it closed in 1991.

Through three location changes and for over one hundred years, one thing remained consistent: crab cakes and other seafood dishes were front and center on the Thompson's menu. According to the *Baltimore Sun*, at a May 1894 party at the restaurant, the menu consisted of "a breakfast of soft crabs, fish, fried chicken, beefsteak, muffins and coffee." The party guests were local brew masters and their families, who got together for an annual celebration that included food and several hours of "rambling about the grounds and along the river shore." The restaurant was even a trendsetter; it was, reportedly, the first restaurant in the country to serve crab imperial. The iconic dish appeared on the menu in the late nineteenth century.

Thompson's was frequently mentioned in local publications for more than its food; the Sea Girt House was often referenced as a landmark in articles reporting on maritime weather.

From 1907 to 1936, the restaurant was owned by August Hennegan, though it retained the name "Thompson." It was popular during those years, and the surrounding neighborhood included attractions like the Riverview amusement park and two racetracks. In a 1964 letter to the editor of the *Sun*, Green Spring Avenue resident John A. Stauch reminisced about childhood visits to the Sea Girt House, when his father would hire a horse and buggy to carry the family through Canton to the restaurant. "Entering the dining room, you were impressed by its openness; all four sides were screened, cool breezes off the water set the hanging Chinese chimes tinkling. The white-clothed tables were ready, and the formally attired waiters vied to serve you," Stauch wrote. He remembered a regular waiter, named Homer, trying deviled crab for the first time, and huge glasses of lemonade and shaved ice, garnished with slices of orange and extra red cherries. Staunch recalled that meals at the restaurant were served family style. He wrote of "hot or cold clam juice, crab soup with half crabs in the bowl, big crab cakes, whole fish—head and tail intact." Stauch said he ate soft crabs ("bigger than your hand") and remembered that everything was "expertly prepared and seasoned."

Thompson's Sea Girt House in 1966. *Courtesy of Baltimore Museum of Industry.*

Swizzle stick from Thompson's Sea Girt House. *Courtesy of Jan Warrington.*

In 1949, the Sea Girt House made a big move. According to a 1985 article written on the restaurant's one hundredth anniversary: "the land under Thompson's was far too valuable to house a mere eating place." The waterfront land was refashioned into a marine terminal, and the restaurant moved north, to Govans. At that time, the restaurant was owned by George W. Thompson Sr., the great-grandson of the founder, and his wife, Margaret M. Thompson. In 1968, George Thompson died after being stabbed during a robbery at his home. After George's death, his wife continued to operate the restaurant with their son, George Thompson Jr.

Under their ownership, the restaurant earned local accolades, particularly for its crab cakes, and gained national notoriety. The restaurant even began to distribute crab cakes nationwide during the 1970s and early 1980s. It was during those years that Lynette Starleper, a third-generation resident of Idlewylde, a neighborhood just northeast of Govans, became a regular at Thompson's. "Even as a child, our family always used the restaurant for special occasions," she said. Starleper recalled memories of her grandfather coming over and saying, "Get dressed, we're going to the Sea Girt." Years later, Starleper and her mother got in the habit of dining at Thompson's every Friday night. "Since it was every Friday, they'd have a table on hold," she said. Starleper said her preferred order was stuffed shrimp ("broiled, not fried—it was great"), and her mother would always order whatever seafood was in season. Her mother, she said, particularly liked the coddies and the fried oysters.

In 1983, the Thompson family sold the restaurant to Tomas Sanz and Jose Sanza, who had both formerly worked at Tio Pepe, and Bruno Vigo, a former owner of Capriccio in Little Italy. The trio kept the menu's focus on Chesapeake-style seafood preparations, but they also added Spanish and northern Italian dishes to the offerings.

By the late 1980s, culinary preferences in Baltimore had shifted and, though crab cakes remained in fashion, other elements of the Thompson's menu lost some of their luster. A 1987 *Baltimore Sun* review called the crab cakes "delightfully seasoned," and the *Sun's* spring 1989 "Dining Out" guide praised some of the restaurant's more old-fashioned (and richer) dishes, including the banana and hollandaise–topped sole Alcazar and shrimp and crab Norfolk. However, the same 1989 article noted that the restaurant was lacking in some of the finer points, including serving well-cleaned mussels.

When Margaret Thompson and her son sold the restaurant, they retained rights to the name. They opened the Original Thompson's Sea Girt House Restaurant on Eighty-Third Street in Ocean City, Maryland, in 1988. That location, which was never technically associated with the original restaurant by anything other than name, closed in 1997, six years after its Govans predecessor.

"I miss it," said Lynette Starleper. "I really enjoyed it. It brings back a lot of good memories with the family and the food was absolutely stupendous."

2
Connolly's Seafood House

A HARBOR FISH HOUSE
1886–1991

While Connolly's was razed in the early 1990s, the ghosts of the waterfront eatery may still be patrolling Baltimore's Inner Harbor. After all, the family spirits were quite active when the fish shack was still serving its signature fried seafood platters and crab cakes before its sudden closure in 1991. "I saw my grandfather as much after his death as before," said Karene Connolly-Smith of Westminster, the great-granddaughter of restaurant founder Thomas J. Connolly. She was referring to Sterling L. Connolly, who took over the establishment after his father's death. Connolly-Smith, who started helping out at the restaurant when she was in kindergarten, shaping crab cakes, remembered the top flying off a cup holder every time it was empty and "hitting" the staff. She also recalled water faucets turning on and off, the clicking of door keys and even apparitions of deceased relatives serving crabs. "It was one hundred percent haunted," she said.

Despite the ghostly activity, the restaurant at 701 East Pratt Street was very much an attraction for the living. It drew the attentions of celebrities like Liberace and Michael Jackson, as well as local officials, like Mayor William Donald Schaefer, who dined there every Sunday with his mother, Tululu Irene Schaefer. There was also a resident green parrot named Polly who enjoyed being loose in the restaurant and reciting television shows. Polly lived in the restaurant until he was banned by the health department and moved to live out his days at Sterling Connolly's home.

Naomi and Sterling Connolly. *Courtesy of Karene Connolly-Smith and the Connolly family.*

TOM CONNOLLY CO.

— CRABS —

Wholesale Oyster Dealers
Pier 5, Pratt St. - Baltimore-2, Md., - 703 E. Pratt St.
MUlberry 9534

Connolly's card. *Courtesy of Karene Connolly-Smith and the Connolly family.*

Connolly's Seafood House dining room. *Courtesy of Karene Connolly-Smith and the Connolly family.*

The restaurant, a ramshackle, green metal structure, was built over the harbor's wooden Pier 5 and grew from a wholesale seafood business that was started by Thomas Connolly and a partner over one hundred years ago. The restaurant began as a small lunchroom that served oysters and other seafood to passengers of the Tolchester ferry, who were traveling to destinations along the Chesapeake Bay. According to Elizabeth Large from the *Baltimore Sun*, the restaurant was eventually expanded to include a bar, a dining room with "a cracked concrete floor, institutional green walls, [and] long rows of tables" and another dining room with "comfortable seating…[that was] decorated with shells and nets and stuffed fish." In a 1975 critique, Large wrote: "I would as soon say something disparaging about the Washington Monument as complain about the food at Connolly's Seafood House." She also remarked that "fried seafood [did]…seem to be the restaurant's specialty."

Jan Purnell, of Franklintown, and her late husband, Rick Purnell, were longtime diners at Connolly's. "Once I met my husband, I went there a lot," said Purnell, who praised the restaurant's shrimp salad. Her husband worked in a building across the street from Connolly's, making it a convenient stop

Connolly's Seafood House. *Courtesy of Karene Connolly-Smith and the Connolly family.*

for his after-work drinks and meals. "It was a business bar, and the food was great," she said. "You knew everyone who was there." Purnell recalled braving cold winter nights to use the restroom. "The ladies' room was over the water in an add-on [room]," she said. "I did not linger. It was brisk." The Purnells were such fans that, after the restaurant closed, they paid $250 for the neon sign that had been displayed in Connolly's front window, and they hung it in their kitchen, where it remains today. "We were just so tickled to be able to save it," Purnell said. "The building may be gone, but the memories are there."

Ric Cottom, the host of WYPR's show *Your Maryland*, and his wife, Barb, were also frequent customers. "We absolutely loved it," he said. "It had the best seafood in Baltimore. The crabs were wonderful." Ric also said that they particularly enjoyed visiting the restaurant on steamy summer nights, when the beer was served in twenty-two-ounce frosted Pilsner glasses as a refreshing antidote to the muggy weather. Cottom, who lives in Roland Park, remembered that the waitresses wore black dresses with white trim and recalled an incident in which one of the servers, who was smacking her gum, approached the table of a well-dressed couple, who didn't seem familiar with Connolly's. "They asked, 'What's fresh?'" said Cottom with a chuckle. "The waitress responded, 'It's all fresh, hon.'"

Connolly's Seafood House menu.
Courtesy of Karene Connolly-Smith and the Connolly family.

Connolly's was finally torn down as part of Baltimore's harbor revitalization to make way for the Christopher Columbus Center of Marine Research and Exploration. "We were heartbroken when it closed," Cottom said. The Connolly family tried to find another location, but Connolly-Smith said the city properties that were available were too expensive. Today, Mama's on the Half Shell in Canton pays tribute to the "beloved Baltimore waterfront seafood house" by including several commemorative dishes on its menu, under a section called "Connolly's Classics." The entrées include fried jumbo shrimp, fried oysters and crab imperial.

To keep the past alive, Connolly-Smith oversees a Facebook page called "Connolly's Seafood Memories" for former diners and employees. "Before Facebook, everybody scattered to the wind," she said. "I was hoping they would find their way back, and they did."

Connolly-Smith was present when the restaurant was demolished on an unseasonably warm day in October 1991. "When the last wall went down, there was a burst of wind and a rainbow went across," she said. "I guess [it] was meant to be."

3

Horn & Horn

A PLACE FOR EVERYONE
1891–1977

I n 1988, Gilbert Sandler wrote in the *Evening Sun*: "Horn & Horn of East Baltimore Street was a special mix of urban characters and urban ideas at work." Sports gamblers; strippers from the Block, a section of East Baltimore Street known for its burlesque clubs; and City Hall politicians often frequented the twenty-four-hour restaurant. Sandler also wrote in a 1976 article: "Sometimes, so many [people] were trying to get [into the Horn & Horn] at 2 and 4 and 5 in the morning that there was a line at the door." In 1942, the restaurant was no longer open for twenty-four hours a day. Sandler noted: "[When the proprietor] put a sign in the window, 'Closed, 1 a.m. to 7 a.m.,' [he] shooed a procession of mourners out onto the sidewalk."

Horn & Horn management told the *Baltimore Sun* that the hours changed because of a "help" issue, but the eatery continued to feed diners until it closed in 1977—an impressive run for a restaurant that was founded in 1891. It was started by members of the Horn family, and, along the way, the original restaurant succumbed to the Great Fire of 1904. In its place, the Horns constructed an ornate, three-story structure with an arched stone façade and reopened the eatery in 1908. "Otto Simonson, a gifted architect, who was instrumental in rebuilding Baltimore after the 1904 fire, fitted out this restaurant in marble, dark wood, scrolled ironwork and electric lights," wrote Jacques Kelly in a 1996 *Sun* article.

According to the *Sun* in 1942, before Prohibition, the lunchroom had a soda fountain and an oyster bar. The newspaper also reported that "[the

Horn & Horn menu.
Photographer Amy Davis,
Courtesy of Estelle Kahn.

restaurant's] waiters wore white coats, and many had handle-bar mustaches." By the early twentieth century, a brigade of waitresses in tidy black uniforms and light-colored aprons took over. While on duty, the waitresses followed a strict dress code that included such caveats as no eye makeup and no cavities or missing teeth and required them to wear a dress that hung no more than twelve inches from the floor, black oxford shoes, a slip and a bra. Regardless of the women's appearance, Sandler was impressed with their skills, noting: "The waitresses…never wrote down (they carried no pads) even the longest and most complicated of orders and…delivered your order exactly right."

The restaurant's fare included chicken and oyster pot pies, chicken and ham biscuits, pancakes, pecan waffles, homemade ice cream, pastries and the popular Red Ball special—corned beef and cabbage, a boiled new potato, a buttered roll and coffee, tea, or hot chocolate—which cost thirty-five cents in 1934. According to reporter G. Jefferson Price III in a 1977 *Sun* article, the upper floors of the restaurant were "high-ceilinged rooms, surrounded by marble" with solid mahogany tabletops and bentwood chairs.

In 1955, the Horn family sold the restaurant to White Coffee Pot Family Inns Inc. "They tell me this was one of the finest restaurants in the city," said Alan Katz, the son of White Coffee Pot's founder, in a 1987 *Evening Sun* article. Horn & Horn grew into a cafeteria-smorgasbord chain with locations in surrounding counties before rebranding to Cactus Willie's Steak and Buffet Bakery in 1998.

From its earliest days, brothers George, Frank and Joseph Horn oversaw the restaurant, but according to *Baltimore's Bygone Department Stores: Many Happy Returns* by Michael J. Lisicky, they had a disagreement over the menu. "George wanted to offer more seafood, and Joseph disagreed," he wrote. "As a result, Joseph left Baltimore and partnered with Frank Hardart in Philadelphia." In Philadelphia, Joseph established the successful Horn & Hardart chain. "Family, yet separate," said Patrick Ford, the great-great grandnephew of Joseph Horn who has kept track of the family history.

George Horn was a managing partner who was actively involved in the restaurant, while Frank "preferred to travel," Ford said. George Horn and his wife, Christina, had five children: Carl, Joe, John, Rosa and Catherine.

• Today's Suggestions •

Robbins Island Oysters on Half Shell (6)   30
Cherry Stone Clams on Half Shell (6)   20
Clams on Half Shell (6)   25
Cocktail Sauce 5c Extra

Mixed Fruit	10	Tomato Juice Cocktail	05
Chicken Soup	10	English Beef Soup	10

PLATTERS

Chicken Pie en Casserole   25
Breaded Veal Cutlet (Tomato Sauce)
   Creamed Fresh Broccoli, Mashed Potatoes   35
Hot Roast Turkey Sandwich (Giblet Gravy), Filling
   and Cranberry Sauce 35, with Potatoes   40
Roast Young Turkey (Giblet Gravy), Filling
   Cranberry Sauce, Buttered Peas,
   Parsley New Potatoes, Roll and Butter   60
Creamed Chicken and Mushrooms on Toast
   and Fresh String Beans   35
Tenderloin Steak
   Fresh Spinach, Baked Potato   50
Roast Prime Ribs of Beef au Jus
   Fresh Brussels Sprouts, Mashed Potatoes   40
Virginia Baked Ham (Glazed Apples)
   Harvard Beets, Candied Sweet Potatoes   40
Fresh Vegetable Platter: Fried Eggplant, Creamed
Broccoli, Buttered Spinach, Candied Sweet Potatoes,
   Roll and Butter   25

Bread, Rolls or Hot Milk Biscuits, Butter   05

VEGETABLES

Glazed Apples	10	Baked Beans (Pot)	10
Buttered Fresh Spinach	10	Baked Potato, Butter	05
French Fried Potatoes	10	Mashed Potatoes	10
Fresh String Beans	10	Fried Eggplant	10
Harvard Beets	10	Buttered Peas	10
Sauer Kraut	10	Candied Sweet Potatoes	10
Creamed Fresh Broccoli	10	Fresh Brussels Sprouts	10

BEVERAGES

Coffee 05	Cocoa 05		Tea 05
Milk (Bottle) 05	Hot Milk 10		Buttermilk 05
Vienna Chocolate 05		Chocolate Milk 10	

Chocolate Milk Ice Cream Float 15
Gosman's Ginger Ale 10

Sunday, December 15, 1940

Children's Dinners
25c

ROAST PRIME RIB OF BEEF
Mashed Potatoes, Gravy
OR
FRESH VEGETABLE PLATE
Buttered Spinach
Creamed Broccoli
Baked Potato
Buttered Roll

Rice Pudding, Vanilla Sauce
Egg Custard Pie
or Ice Cream

Milk, Vienna Chocolate or Tea

. . . Oysters . . .

Fried (6) 35,	(12)		70
Broiled on Toast (6) 40,	(12)		75
Stew (Small) 30,	(Large)		45
Cream Stew (Small) 45;	(Large)		65
Panned (Small) 30,	(Large)		60
Pan Roast (Small) 35;	(Large)		65

3 Fried Oysters, Pepper Hash 20,
   with French Fried Potatoes   25
Oyster Platter: 3 Fried Oysters,
   Cole Slaw, Sliced Tomato,
   French Fried Potatoes   30

*We Make Our Own Pies, Cakes,
Pastries and Ice Cream*

•

WE ARE NOT RESPONSIBLE FOR
ARTICLES LOST OR STOLEN

SUNDAY DINNERS

Choice

Chilled Fruit Cup
Tomato Juice Cocktail
Cup of Chicken Soup or English Beef Soup

ROAST YOUNG TURKEY, Giblet Gravy	.85
Filling Cranberry Sauce	
TENDERLOIN STEAK	.75
VIRGINIA BAKED HAM (Glazed Apples)	.65
BREADED VEAL CUTLET, Tomato Sauce	.60

Choice of Two Vegetables

Waldorf Salad

Hot Rolls, Bread or Hot Milk Biscuits and Butter

Coffee	Tea	Vienna Chocolate

Choice

Plum Pudding, Sherry and Hard Sauce
Fresh Pumpkin Pie
Chocolate Eclair
Layer Cake or Ice Cream

•

DESSERTS

Hot Apple Dumpling, Vanilla Sauce		10
Baked Apple 10;	with Cream	15
Chocolate Whipped Cream Layer Cake		10
Fruit Gelatine, Whipped Cream		10
Plum Pudding, Sherry and Hard Sauce		10
Whipped Cream Eclair 10	Cup Custard	10
Glazed Apples, Cream 10	Chocolate Eclair	10
	Cocoanut Layer Cake	10

PIES: Fresh Apple, Fresh Pumpkin, Hot Mince
   or Egg Custard   10
SUNDAES: Chocolate Fudge, Maple Pecan, Pineapple 15
ICE CREAM: Vanilla, Chocolate, Butter Pecan   10

Above: Horn & Horn menu items.
Photographer Amy Davis, courtesy of Estelle Kahn.

Right: Rosa Horn, the daughter of founder
George Horn. *Courtesy of Patrick Ford.*

After George passed away, Carl and Joe took over, and Carl eventually assumed responsibility, Ford said. Rosa and her other siblings were restaurant shareholders, though not active participants.

Gilbert Sandler called Horn & Horn "easily the most popular all-night restaurant in Baltimore well into the 1970s....There were no successful imitations, before or since."

4
Women's Industrial Exchange

TOMATO ASPIC AND DEVILED EGGS
EARLY 1900s–2014

I'll have the tomato aspic, please."

It's a line that was surely heard countless times during the century that the restaurant at the Women's Industrial Exchange operated out of its North Charles Street home. The dish—a jellied tomato sauce concoction—is the epitome of old-fashioned and the Exchange.

The Women's Industrial Exchange was founded by a Quaker woman named G. Harmon Brown, along with eleven other women, in July 1880. The organization opened to the public in October that year and originally operated out of Brown's home on West Saratoga Street. The purpose of the Exchange was to provide a place for women to sell handmade goods anonymously in order to avoid any embarrassment about the need to do so. The consignors were often well-heeled women who wanted to avoid the stigma of working. A day after the official opening of the Exchange, on October 16, 1880, the *Baltimore Sun* released a statement: "The object of the society is to supply a long-felt want by increasing opportunity for the support of women who are dependent upon their own exertions, and to assist those who wish to help themselves."

The restaurant didn't become part of the operation until after 1899, when the Exchange moved to its current home at the corner of Charles and Pleasant Streets. "My understanding is that the restaurant was built out when they had the boardinghouse," said acting Women's Exchange board president Jenny Hope. "The house was built as a private residence in 1815, and they added onto it in the early 1900s…I think they added on the dining room for the boarders. They realized at some point that they could

Women's Industrial Exchange. *Courtesy of Kit Pollard.*

run a restaurant and started serving breakfast and lunch." Though the exact details around the opening of the lunchroom are murky, by the mid-1930s, it was busy and growing. According to board meeting notes, in January 1937, the restaurant served 6,564 customers and made a profit of $624.20.

Above and opposite: Women's Industrial Exchange board meeting notes from February 1937 (*above*) and November 1936 (*opposite*) that show total sales and customers served. *Courtesy of Jenny Hope.*

The restaurant's layout was somewhat unusual; it had an entrance-level dining room at the back of the building, a downstairs room with a bar and a lower-level kitchen. "It was a bustling kitchen, but it was small. It seemed like a well-oiled machine," said Hope. Food and handwritten orders were shuttled between the floors via a tin can attached to a pully system.

The main level dining room's iconic look received much praise over the years. "The dining room in [the] back is a time machine into the genteel past: black-and-white tile floor, long red banquette, cream-colored walls hung with soothing pictures of birds and flowers," wrote Michael and Jane Stern in a 1987 *Baltimore Sun* article. The basement, with its serpentine counter, was famous as well. "I thought it was the coolest thing since sliced bread," said John Shields, co-owner of Gertrude's in the Baltimore Museum of Art and former Exchange diner. "The counter weaved in and out. It was an architectural marvel, that counter." The downstairs area was also known for being a meeting place for a core group of customers: a handful of men who dubbed themselves the "Down Under Club." In a 1985 *Baltimore Sun* article, Isaac Rehert described the club as a mix of "lawyers, merchants, manufacturers, judges, librarians, sea captains—even once, the Australian ambassador" who met, informally, for lunch and were always served by their favorite waitress: Mrs. Phyllis Sanders. The atmosphere, Rehert said, had "so much jocularity that, for a new customer, it is hard to separate the truth from the quips."

November 1934

The regular meeting of the Board of Managers
of the Woman's Ind. Exchange was held on
November 10, with the president presiding
the following members were present:—
Mrs. Davis.   Mrs. Trimble   Mrs. Tucker
Mrs. Barton   Mrs. Warner
Mrs. Harvey   Mrs. Moser
The minutes were read and approved—
The Treasurer, Mrs. Harvey, reported a balance
Nov. 1 of $721.10.—
Mrs. Warner read the store report which
showed a deficit of $32.67.
Mrs. Moser read the lunch room report
which showed a balance for the month of
$391.32—The profit for the month was
$893.37, 8241 customers were served.

From the waitresses to the doorman and the kitchen crew, the Exchange staff members were known for their extreme competence and loyalty. In 1995, the *Baltimore Sun*'s Jacques Kelly interviewed several Exchange waitresses. At the time, the youngest waitress was in her fifties, but more than half the women on staff were eighty years old or older. Decked out in crisp blue dresses, with aprons tied in giant white bows, the waitresses cut impressive figures as they efficiently made their way around the dining room. Possibly the best-known of the waitresses was "Miss Margeurite" Schertle. Schertle, who lived to be one hundred years old, died in 2001, just five years after retiring from the Exchange, where she had worked for almost fifty years. Her twin sister, Anna Schertle, worked alongside her for many of those years. The pair also married brothers and lived next door to one another in Hamilton. In Miss Margeurite's obituary, longtime Exchange customer, former state senator and member of the Down Under Club Julian "Jack" Lapides said of Schertle, "What an alert, sparkling, feisty and marvelous person she was. She took nothing off nobody—she was courteous and polite—but she didn't back off." Schertle's fame even expanded beyond city lines. She had a cameo in the film *Sleepless in Seattle* that shot a few scenes at the Exchange. In the film, she is the waitress who serves the characters played by Meg Ryan and Rosie O'Donnell. Schertle reportedly gave the crew a bit of her trademark sass when they asked her to play the role a certain way. She responded by saying, "Do me a favor. Let me do it my way."

Change was never going to be the Exchange's strong suit. "The only thing we can't do is change anything. We'd get letters of protest," said the then–board head, Conradt "Connie" Boyce Whitescarver, to Jacques Kelly in 1995. "We keep it so people can remember Baltimore the way it was." Like its décor, the menu at the Exchange was not something to be tinkered with on a regular basis—if ever—and that was the way the customers liked it. "Cuisine is not the whole of the Exchange's appeal, but it's not the least of it either," wrote Lynn Williams in the *Baltimore Sun's* 1990 dining guide. "This is the kind of food once consumed in department store tearooms, or at bridal showers. Ladylike. Definitely unexotic." John Shields was also one of the Exchange's creatures of habit. "I'd always get the same thing—an egg salad sandwich," he said. "But I would get the tomato aspic if I had other people there, because that's what everybody talked about." The tomato aspic, along with the chicken salad, deviled eggs and desserts, including homemade cakes, pies and Charlotte Russe, were the most famous dishes at the Exchange. They're still the dishes former patrons miss the most.

By the mid-1990s, longtime waitresses of the Exchange began to observe some shifts in the restaurant's business. Their lunch crowd, which was once comprised of "debutantes and their mothers," had evolved into one of businessmen and women who were dropping in for a break from work. Other subtle changes included the disappearance of finger bowls and a shift from homemade mayonnaise to jarred. While the tearoom was beloved, it wasn't consistently profitable. The need to raise funds was a constant over the years. "There's a 1917 book done by the board, a program for a fundraiser they had when the building was in dire straits," said Jenny Hope. "You could write this over and over every decade. They needed to raise money to pay off the mortgage."

Throughout the years, the tearoom was occasionally in the black, but, by 1995, proceeds from the handmade clothing and crafts sold in the gift shop, as well as rent payments from the upstairs apartment and ground floor retail space "[helped] compensate for the losses incurred by the luncheon tomato aspic and chicken salads," according to a *Sun* article by Jacques Kelly.

In more recent years, the Exhange experimented with bringing outside groups in to operate the lunchroom. From December 2003 to January 2005, the tearoom was operated by Roslyn DuPree. Shortly after the restaurant closed in 2005, the board decided to temporarily close the shop as well. At the time, the president of the volunteer board, Helen Weiss, called the shop's closing "a bump in the road" and promised to reopen "bigger and better, and brighter and shinier." Weiss also reported that multiple restaurateurs were interested in reviving the tearoom's operation. "The chicken salad will be back!" she told the *Sun*.

It did come back, but never permanently. Jerry Edwards, now the president of Chef's Expressions, took over for a short time, followed by Galen and Bridget Sampson, who, at the time, were operating the Hampden restaurant Dogwood. In 2011, Irene Smith, the owner of the Souper Freak food truck, took over the space and introduced an old-fashioned menu. For a few years, Smith's efforts were successful, but in June 2014, the restaurant closed again.

These days, the Exchange restaurant isn't open, but you can grab breakfast or lunch at Jack & Zach's, a small diner that Zachary Schoettler operates out of the Exchange building. Plus, there's a new plan in the works to run the kitchen as a commissary space, where people can do food prep for food-related businesses, like food trucks.

There may not be any tomato aspic available today at the corner of Charles and Pleasant, but the spirit of the tearoom, as a place where Baltimoreans can come together to remember the past and support one another, lives on.

5
Miller Bros.

A FAVORITE MEETING PLACE
1912–1980s

K nown as "the place to eat" by its regulars and anyone-who-was-anyone passing through Baltimore, Miller Bros. Restaurant was at the top of the Baltimore restaurant game for a big chunk of the early and mid-twentieth century. Located at 119 West Fayette Street downtown, in a space big enough to seat 450 people, the restaurant got its start in 1912, when it was purchased by, as its name suggests, a pair of brothers named Miller.

John Henry "Harry" and Fred Miller grew up in Washington, D.C., where their father, Charles Miller, ran a restaurant near the FBI building. The Millers, two sons in a family of five, grew up in D.C., but they had roots in Baltimore: their grandparents, George and Elizabeth Miller, lived in the city. Harry and Fred reclaimed those roots when they moved back to Baltimore and purchased a restaurant called Schneider's Old German Café. They initially renamed the restaurant to Miller Brothers German Café, but the name was later shortened to Miller Bros. Restaurant.

Even in the restaurant's early days, Miller Bros.'s cuisine was never strictly German. A menu from September 8, 1942, lists a wide variety of dishes, some of which are still common finds on Baltimore menus. The only difference is that today's diners can only wish to pay sixty-five cents for a crab cake (made with "back fin lump only") paired with coleslaw. Other recommendations from the chefs, like boiled beef and potato for seventy-five cents, haven't proved as classic. During the winter, wild game was often on the menu, and, if they got lucky, diners might see a moose, elk, deer or bear

Miller Bros. dining room in 1967. *Courtesy of the Baltimore Museum of Industry.*

Miller Bros. kitchen in 1967. *Courtesy of Baltimore Museum of Industry.*

carcass outside the restaurant a day or two prior to a new dish in the dining room. Turtle soup was another memorable specialty.

In 1975, the *Baltimore Sun* published an article reminiscing about the good old days of Miller Bros. The writer, Edward C. Wiscott, listed a few of his favorite dishes, which included oysters from the raw bar, oyster stew, served with "a tiny floating red crab," seafood platters, Welsh rarebit, Liederkranz cheese and raw beef and onion served on black rye bread. The rye bread, which was made by the restaurant's own bakery, made its way into other Baltimore restaurants and even into private homes; it was delivered by the Miller brothers' own delivery trucks. Wiscott effusively praised the restaurant's service and food but added, "above and beyond them there was a pervading spirit, a warmth, a genuine friendliness I have never seen in any other restaurant."

Miller Bros.'s first floor was generously proportioned; that's where most of the dining happened. But on the second floor, there was a room available for a loose club of democratic politicos known as the "Round Table," who held daily lunches at the restaurant. During these meetings, they would discuss politics as well as other matters of import, including baseball and religion. According to Wiscott, the Miller Bros.'s bar also had a group of lunchtime regulars, the "Barflies," who were such an integral part of the restaurant that Harry Miller hosted annual Christmas parties for them and gifted members of the group with gold lapel pins in the shape of house flies.

During its heyday, Miller Bros. was the place to be seen. Anyone traveling through Baltimore, from athletes to actresses, stopped by during their visits. Federal Bureau of Investigation (FBI) director J. Edgar Hoover was a regular, visiting during horse racing season. Miller Bros. even got a mention in Leon Uris's 1958 historical fiction novel about Israel's founding, *Exodus*. In the book, the character Bill Fry, a Mossad captain tasked with finding, outfitting and captaining a ship to transport five thousand refugees from France, dines on Miller Bros.'s clam chowder as he ponders his task. With pop culture references and so many luminaries coming through its doors, Miller Bros. was often in the spotlight, and, in the early 1960s, when both Baltimore and the country as a whole were in the throes of the civil rights movement, not all of the attention it received was flattering.

In August 1961, the restaurant found itself caught in the middle of the movement when a trio of reporters from the *Baltimore AFRO-American* newspaper dressed in traditional African garb and posed as diplomats. They were seated and served without incident, but had they arrived in their everyday clothes, they would have been turned away. The reporters used the

Miller Bros. menu from 1941. *Courtesy of the Rare Book Division of the New York Public Library. Retrieved from www.digitalcollections.nypl.org.*

experience to highlight the disparity with which black diplomats and black Baltimoreans would be treated during a time of segregation. That wasn't the only time Miller Bros. was on the front lines of civil rights strife.

A 1962 report on Baltimore's progress, in terms of racial equality, published by the Sidney Hollander Foundation, reported that in February of that year, Miller Bros. refused to serve a table of white leaders of Christian and Jewish communities because their party included Dr. Furman Templeton, the African American executive director of the Baltimore Urban League. The restaurant also gained national notoriety in 1962, when legendary composer, conductor and performer Leonard Bernstein stopped in Baltimore during a tour. After being told that one of his party, a violinist, would not be served because he was black, Bernstein raised eyebrows by walking out.

By the time these scandals hit the restaurant, it was no longer in the hands of the original Miller brothers. Fred had died in 1931, and his immediate family withdrew their involvement in the restaurant after his death (his son and wife would later open the Kingsville Inn, which closed in 1970). Harry continued running the restaurant until his death in 1958; at which point, his wife and son took over its management.

In 1963, just after Bernstein's dramatic visit, the area around Miller Bros.'s Fayette Street location was in transition due to the development of Charles Center. On June 30, 1963, the restaurant served its last meal at its original location; the building where it was located was torn down as part of the development project.

A few years later, Miller Bros. reopened in the Statler Hilton, a hotel that had been built on the same stretch of Fayette Street where the original Miller Bros. operated. (Since then, the hotel has changed hands several times; it's now a Radisson.) After its reopening, and without the family at the helm, Miller Bros. never regained its luster. In his January 1972 review of the reopened restaurant, *Baltimore Sun* restaurant critic John Dorsey urged his fellow Baltimoreans to stop comparing the restaurant to the Miller Bros. of old and instead to take it on its own merits. "Perhaps because of memories of the old place, Miller's seems to have a much worse reputation around town than, to me, it deserves," he wrote.

By the mid-1980s, though, even Dorsey had changed his tune. The revamped Miller Bros. was closed by then, and Dorsey wrote, in a review of the restaurant that replaced it, that the hotel version of the once iconic spot was a "travesty on the name Miller Bros."

6
Hutzler's Colonial Tea Room

REFINED DEPARTMENT STORE DINING
1917–1984

As a little boy, John Shields—now the co-owner of Gertrude's in the Baltimore Museum of Art—often tagged along with his mother when she went on shopping trips to the Hutzler Brothers department store. At that time, the store was located in the "Palace," a grand Art Deco building on Howard Street. For Shields, the highlights of the day were his frequent trips in the manned elevator. He said he also has fond memories of lunching with his mother in the store's sixth-floor Colonial Tea Room. "It seemed like the epitome of high-class society," he recalled. "They had the finger bowls, they had the beautiful china, the waitresses were dressed in these beautiful uniforms. As a kid, you thought you had died and gone to heaven when you went there."

Hutzler's was founded in 1858 by Abram Hutzler with the help of his father, Moses. The first store was opened at the corner of Howard and Clay Streets in downtown Baltimore, and, in 1888, the Hutzler Brothers Palace Building was built on Howard Street. Over the next several decades, the building was expanded and updated; by the middle of the twentieth century, it was a large and impressive presence downtown. The store itself was a popular destination right away, but the Colonial Tea Room wasn't part of the Hutzler's experience for several years. It opened on the fourth floor of the Palace in 1917 and remained in that location until December 1942, when it opened in a new spot on the sixth floor.

From the start, the Colonial Tea Room was a hit. According to Michael J. Lisicky's book, *Hutzler's: Where Baltimore Shops,* on the Tea Room's opening

Hutzler's Palace Building. *Courtesy of Eli Pousson from the Baltimore Heritage organization.*

day, more than one thousand people dined there. Over the years, it was a popular destination for shopping women, local businessmen and politicians, like Mayor William Donald Schaefer. For decades, the Tea Room also served as a venue for fashion shows—all the better to encourage lunching ladies to continue shopping—and for gatherings like sorority founders' day events and luncheons for wives tagging along with their husbands for college reunions.

The Tea Room's menu included sandwiches, soups and entrees, including terrapin stew—long after it had been struck from most local menus—and chicken chow mein. The restaurant called its potato chips Saratoga chips—a nod to Hutzler's Saratoga Street location and to Saratoga Springs, New York, where the chips were invented—and many of the sandwiches were served on cheese bread that was also available for purchase, by the loaf, from the store's bakery.

Longtime Baltimorean Betti Sheldon visited the Tea Room with her mother. She was a particular fan of the Tea Room's cheese bread and club sandwiches, as well as the overall atmosphere. "Those were the days," she said. "Even my mother talked about everyone wearing hats and gloves. I was a little girl and thought it was so elegant." The Tea Room's formal atmosphere, with its mahogany chairs and linens on the tables, was accented by deep red hurricane lamps and waitresses dressed in crisp gray-and-white uniforms. "The cooking was plain but served with enough flourish and style to make it distinctive," wrote *Baltimore Sun* reporter Jacques Kelly in a 1995 remembrance of the restaurant. "Many an entrée was served with carrot-gelatin mold, as if the chef thought you needed to eat something healthy that day."

The Hutzler's building was also home to other dining options, including the Saratoga Street bakery (famous for the cheese bread and its decadent cakes), a basement luncheonette that opened in 1929, and the Quixie, a lower-priced restaurant on the sixth floor, which was open from 1942 to 1972. Like many department stores, Hutzler's success led to expansion plans. The company enlarged the Palace building several times and opened additional stores throughout the region; the first was a Towson location that opened in 1952. The Towson store also had a bakery and a tearoom, called the Valley View Room. Like the downtown Tea Room, Towson's third-floor restaurant frequently hosted fashion shows and was considered a fun place to dine while shopping. It was a popular spot with a lovely view of the Hampton mansion, but it wasn't quite as refined as the downtown location. "I went to Towson for a lot of different things," said Betti Sheldon. "It wasn't as elegant or intimate, but it was still a nice place to go and take the kids."

In the 1970s, as the city's demographics changed and lifestyles and shopping behaviors evolved, the company began to struggle. By 1977, sales at the downtown store were half what they'd been nine years earlier, in 1968. In 1980, Harborplace opened at the Inner Harbor, drawing shoppers farther away from Howard Street.

Even in its waning years, the Tea Room never lost its gentility. As an adult, John Shields continued to visit the Tea Room, lunching there several times a week during the mid-1970s. "It was fading a bit," he said. "But it still had this old-world kind of charm." In 1983, *Baltimore Sun* reporter Tom Nugent wrote that the Tea Room "hasn't lost its charm in recent years," thanks, in part, to staff like Theresa Ryan, who had waited tables in the Tea Room since 1958. The "Hutzler way," Ryan told Nugent, involves "finesse, graciousness, politeness, pleasantness, and above all, patience." Plus, she said, "the clientele is *class* and it's a pleasure dealing with them."

By the 1970s and 1980s, the clientele may have still been "class," but it was also aging. In a 1973 *Baltimore Sun* review, restaurant critic John Dorsey admitted that he thought of the Tea Room as a "matron's restaurant," citing the artificial flowers and paper doilies on the tables and the lunchtime fashion shows geared toward middle-aged ladies.

During the 1980s, the Colonial Tea Room was collateral damage as management made changes in an attempt to stay relevant. In 1984, Hutzler's president Angelo Arena moved store operations out of the original Palace Building, where the Tea Room was located, into a smaller building nearby, as part of a five-year plan to grow from eight to fifteen Baltimore area stores. Unfortunately, Arena's five-year plan was not a success. In 1987, the company began shutting down locations. The Towson location was the last store standing; it, too, closed in 1990, but not before cost-cutting changes impacted the menu at the Valley View Room. The restaurant was forced to cut corners, buying premade pie crusts, using cheaper ingredients in the blue cheese salad dressing and scrapping the Jell-O that traditionally came with its chicken pot pie.

Hutzler's Palace Building was added to the National Register of Historic Places in 1984. In the same year, the City of Baltimore purchased the Palace Building and renovated it for use by the city's Department of Human Resources. Local telecommunications company AiNET purchased the building, along with its next-door neighbor, in 2014. Today, the building houses underground servers that process about 25 percent of global internet traffic. It is high tech inside, but its historic façade remains on the outside, standing as a proud nod to the glory days of Hutzler's and the Colonial Tea Room, with its finger bowls, cheese toast sandwiches and lunching ladies in hats and gloves.

7

The Southern Hotel

A POSH DINING ROOM
1918–1964

On the final night of dinner service at the Southern Hotel, the glamorous fourteen-story building that graced the corner of Light and Redwood Streets in downtown Baltimore, guests dined on broiled rockfish from the Chesapeake Bay, crab cakes and curried lamb. It was "steamboat-pure Maryland," according to a *Baltimore Sun* article lamenting the closing of the hotel and its dining room. The Southern was known, during its heyday, as one of the city's poshest spots to dine, dance and stay.

The Southern Hotel's location had a strong and alluring history of hospitality. Previously, the site was the home of the Fountain Inn, a spot frequented by George Washington. Later, it became the Carrollton Hotel, which was destroyed in the Great Baltimore Fire of 1904. The Southern Hotel's cornerstone was laid on March 26, 1917; it opened for business just under a year later, on March 7, 1918. When it finally did open, Baltimoreans—and those from farther afield—flocked there. Notable guests of the hotel, and likely its restaurant, included several presidents, including both Roosevelts, William Howard Taft, Warren G. Harding, Herbert Hoover, and Calvin Coolidge, and captains of industry like William Randolph Hearst and John D. Rockefeller Jr. Even legendary illusionist Harry Houdini stopped in for a stay.

The building's financier, Abraham J. Fink, was still in his twenties when he opened the hotel, but the Mount Washington resident had already "made several fortunes," according to a 1999 Frederick Rasmussen article in the

Baltimore Sun. Fink was a mover and shaker, and he was not afraid to make waves. Case in point: when the hotel opened in 1918, it employed women as elevator operators and front desk rooming clerks; these were jobs that, until then, had been the domain of men.

Inside the hotel, guests and those stopping in had several dining options, including a basement cafeteria that served quick meals and a dining room that played host to both dramatic evening meals and many a business deal. From its start, the hotel drew an elegant crowd. In a 1918 article describing the opening reception, the *Sun* reported that the hotel's rooms were filled for the night and that "women in gorgeous gowns flocked to the hotel with their escorts and enjoyed the dinner that was provided in the main dining room."

On New Year's Eve 1925, the hotel hosted a whopping two thousand guests, who dined on "a dinner of lobster bisque, breast of guinea hen, Smithfield ham and mushrooms, sweet potato souffle, salad, ice cream and coffee from the hotel's green-and-white monogrammed dinnerware," according to a 1986 *Baltimore Sun* article by Jacques Kelly. The cost? Six dollars per person. The hotel hosted many special dinners throughout its time in the spotlight, including a 1936 event in honor of Hans Schuler, the then-president of the Maryland Institute College of Art. Presented by the School Art League of Baltimore City, the meal included potage Florentine, stuffed Long Island duckling, applesauce, cauliflower hollandaise, sweet potato glace and a salad of lettuce, apricot and cream cheese with French dressing.

A rooftop club, originally called the Southern Roof but later renamed the Spanish Villa, was a bona fide roof garden, decked out with canvas awnings and trellises. The Spanish Villa quickly became *the* place to be seen in early twentieth-century Baltimore. "The cognoscenti dined and danced and took in the view of the harbor from 12 stories up," wrote the *Baltimore Sun's* Gilbert Sandler in a 1982 article. Sandler tracked down the club's former maître d', Walter Kloetzi, who reminisced, saying, "We were out in the open, there was dancing under the stars. On moonlit summer evenings, you could dine by the dance floor, look up and see the moon and the stars, look down and see the Inner Harbor and the twinkling lights of the bay excursion boats." The view at the time, of course, would be a much less developed one than it is today—more a working harbor than one dotted with hotels, restaurants, museums and the tourists they draw. Kloetzi recalled local celebrities like Governor Ritchie, Mayor Broening and Mayor Jackson as frequent guests, and said the band—Lou Becker's Orchestra—opened and closed each evening with the song "In a Little

Southern Hotel menu, 1947. *Courtesy of Kit Pollard.*

Spanish Town." The club was open from 1925 to 1940, though the hotel restaurant remained open until the closing of the hotel in 1964.

The fortunes of the hotel took a downward turn following Abraham Fink's death in 1963. On December 10, 1964, the hotel—which appeared to be a going concern—closed abruptly. Three years later, it was purchased by the Maritime Engineers Beneficial Association, and, from then until 1984, it housed the downtown campus of the Calhoon Engineering School, a maritime engineering school.

Long after the hotel's closing, rumors about its "resurrection"—and proposals for how that might look—continued to swirl. Developers presented options for demolition and rebirth, while preservationists made the case that the historic building should be revitalized. For a time, it appeared it would become an upscale home for senior living. According to Richard Rymland, a developer behind a senior living proposal put forth in the mid-1980s, the hotel's history as a swank spot for dining and dancing was part of its potential draw. In a 1986 article, he told the *Baltimore Sun* that many of his clients—those over sixty-five years old—had good memories of their times at the Spanish Villa. "When you say the Southern Hotel to these people, they all know what you're talking about," he said.

While plans for senior living never came to fruition, ultimately, the developers won out over preservationists; the hotel was demolished in 1999. For years, the site was used only for parking until 2016, when developer Madison Marquette started construction, turning nearly the whole block into a mixed-use office and residential complex called One Light Street.

The twenty-eight-story, glass-walled building is topped with an outdoor space including a pool, common area and dog park. But, could it possibly be as glamorous as the Spanish Villa in its heyday? It's hard to imagine.

8

Martick's Restaurant Francais

BOHEMIAN VIBE WITH A DOORBELL
1920s–2008

Baltimoreans have never been able to resist a character, and Morris Martick, the proprietor of the Mulberry Street French restaurant that bore his name, was a character of the highest order. He was an eccentric, an entertainer, a chef committed to his craft (and to finding the cheapest ingredients around) and a boss described both as "like a father" and "bordering on abusive." In a letter to the editor of the *Baltimore Sun*, following Martick's passing in 2011, Towson resident Donald W. Strauss wrote that he was "a gem of genuine Baltimore culture. His restaurant was a mirror of the man: always elegant, yet the polar opposite of pretentious."

Morris Martick was born in the early 1920s, on the second floor of the Mulberry Street building that would later become his restaurant. His parents, Harry and Florence, were immigrants from Poland, and Morris was one of five children. The family operated a grocery and a street-level bar out of the building. During Prohibition, they also sold liquor, which got them in hot water. At one point, Harry Martick spent a year in jail for selling to undercover officers.

After Morris graduated from City College high school, he took over the bar, and it became a go-to spot for Baltimore's bohemian, artsy crowd. It attracted well-known jazz acts, including Billie Holiday, and large crowds. Martick was also an artist in his own right—a Dadaist in the truest sense of the word. Back in the mid-1960s, he framed an old, dust-stained piece of cardboard that had been covering a hole in the men's room and entered it in the annual, juried "Life of Baltimore" exhibit at the Peale Museum.

The piece, which he called "Dust Horses—Photo Finish," was selected by the judges for inclusion in the exhibit. For a brief time, he was also an aspiring politician. In 1966, Morris threw his hat in the ring for the House of Delegates seat in the first legislative district. He campaigned on a "Serves You Right" ticket. "If you vote for me, it serves you right," he told the *Sun*. His candidacy was not successful, but it did add to his lore.

For several decades, Martick ran the bar, welcoming everyone from college kids to members of the LGBT community. But he still wasn't content. In 1967, sick of his artsy and often poor clientele, Martick closed up shop and absconded for the rural French town of Pacy-sur-Eure. There, he worked in a small country restaurant, learning the ins and outs of French country cooking. Armed with that knowledge, he returned to Baltimore, redecorated the restaurant and reopened in 1970.

When he reopened, he put a bell on the door, which he kept locked, and patrons had to ring it to gain entry. Rumor has it that the bell was a throwback to the restaurant's speakeasy days, but, according to Jimmy Rouse, a Martick's waiter for seven years who later went on to open Louie's Bookstore Café, it never really was a speakeasy, just a place where people could buy liquor. And the bell? "It was so he could keep out the old clientele," said Rouse. "He wanted to make it fancy, so they couldn't be there because they didn't have any money, the artists."

"The décor was eccentric," said Rouse. "He had surplus airplane tin riveted to the walls on one side, and the other side had this snakeskin wallpaper." There was also a big folk-art statue of a "bread lady" that Martick bought at an antique store in Pennsylvania and little stained-glass windows. The restaurant where Martick had worked in France was on a stream and served trout en bleu using fish caught from the stream. To replicate this in the city, he put a big fish tank in the dining room and stocked it with trout, so guests could choose the specific fish they wanted for dinner.

In the *Baltimore Sun's* 1980 dining guide, critic John Dorsey wrote that, in 1970, when Martick's opened as a restaurant, it was the only French place in Baltimore City. "It was a nice try, but it was too chancy," he wrote. "You could have a good meal or an awful one." In the ten years following the restaurant's opening, French cuisine had become more of a staple in the city, Dorsey wrote, and the increased competition meant that Martick had to up his game. He did that, according to Dorsey and others. "Martick's has always been good to very good, even excellent," wrote Dan Rodricks in a 2002 *Baltimore Sun* column. Patrons' favorite dishes included the bouillabaisse, salmon Florentine, beef burgundy, the

Martick's dining room. *Courtesy of Historic American Buildings Survey.*

country paté and a sweet potato soup that was frequently dubbed the city's best.

When Morris Martick hired Jimmy Rouse in 1974, it was out of desperation; that's a common story from former Martick's employees:

> *I was sitting in the Mount Royal Tavern, and this guy comes in, who works behind the bar, and said, "I just got fired from my day job. I threw a bottle at the owner."* He said he worked at Martick's, and I [thought], *there must be a job opening. So, I went down there and he hired me on the spot. That* [was] *often how Morris hired—spur of the moment and desperately.*

Rouse worked lunch and dinner shifts, giving him an up-close and personal look at Martick's schedule. The chef shopped for ingredients twice every day, once in the morning for lunch and again in the afternoon for dinner. He was always on the hunt for the cheapest ingredients he could find, said Rouse, but he made magic with them. "Morris was really good at figuring out how to make gourmet food with the cheapest ingredients possible," he said. "Everybody raved about his salad dressing, but he used cheap vinegar, not extra virgin olive oil and just garlic in a blender with salt and pepper. It was a really simple dressing, but excellent. He had a good sense of proportion."

Going to market was also his primary source of social interaction, since he both lived and worked in the Martick's building. "He lived on the third floor, in the attic," remembered Rouse. "He had a little cot up there and there was this circuitous path to the cot between all his junk antiques and dirty laundry. He didn't really have any friends; his whole social life was the suppliers he'd go visit and the people in his restaurant." His quirkiness was apparent to the restaurant's guests, too. "He would often wander down into the dining room and people would call him over and [ask], 'What do you recommend?' Morris's response would be, 'Well, I recommend you try another restaurant,'" said Rouse, laughing at the memory.

John Shields, now the owner of Gertrude's in the Baltimore Museum of Art, lived across the street from Martick's for a time. His memories of the place are vivid and surreal. "You could've been in a Fellini film," he said. "It was not like a restaurant. You were in an alternate universe paradigm. You never knew what was going to happen." Shields's favorite dishes were the bouillabaisse and the paté, though, when he was living nearby, his budget more often kept him to green salad rather than an extravagant meal. Either way, he loved it. "[The restaurant] had this nouvelle Paris feel to it that was almost animated," he said. "Morris was a character. When he was holding court, he was the master of that universe."

Tonya Thomas, now the general manager at Ida B's Table, worked in the kitchen at Martick's for about six months in 2006. "A lot of people told me I was one of the few people who worked there that long," she said. "I learned a lot from him—the dishes he'd become known for. People loved his peach bread pudding, his sweet potato soup, bouillabaisse, lamb chops, pork loin." Thomas admits that she was one of the employees who escaped his wrath. "He could be difficult to work with. He would fuss at people, call people a dummy—but he never called me that. [Sometimes] on the line, he would get crazy," she said.

Rouse, who also described his relationship with Martick as a good one, has similar memories. "Morris was hard on people," he said. "When he decided he was going to ride somebody, he would ride them mercilessly. He had this sense of who was vulnerable. So, a lot of people, he rode right out of the restaurant in short order."

When Martick turned eighty in 2003, the community that came out to fête him at his birthday party, held at the Creative Alliance, was as boisterous and eclectic as his restaurant. Former employees, customers and friends gathered, regaling one another with stories and even a poem about the great memories they had of the restaurant in its heyday. And the not-so-great memories, which, over time, seemed to mellow to fond remembrances more than anything else. "At first, I hated his guts," said former employee Katie Brennan, according to the *Baltimore Sun*. "Then it became a challenge—how far can I push him. Then, you end up loving him." Later, she said, "He was crazy as a bedbug, but he was a great boss. He worked every shift and worked just as hard or harder than anyone there."

Like Rouse, Tom DiVenti was hanging out at Mount Royal Tavern when he heard Martick's was looking for help. He started in the kitchen and worked there for five years. "Morris was a true original Baltimore character who gave others the freedom to be characters too," DiVenti wrote in a recollection of his time at the restaurant. "It was a beautiful dysfunctional family. In the five years of my apprenticeship there, I viewed Martick's as my sanctuary, refuge and sustenance. Morris was the father many of us never had."

Martick's closed in 2008, and Morris died in 2011. Since then, there have been whispers that the restaurant would reopen in some form. In 2013, Morris's brother, Alex, along with his nephew and another partner, took steps to open a speakeasy-style bar in the space, but it never fully materialized. In 2019, the development group Park Avenue Partners received permission from Baltimore's Commission for Historic and Architectural Preservation (CHAP) to tear down the back portion of the Martick's building, while preserving the front third, including its façade. The proposed development includes retail and a six-story apartment building. The decision to preserve the building came after former Martick's employees and fans spearheaded efforts to keep it as a landmark. According to a Baltimore magazine article about the proposed redevelopment, during a demolition hearing with CHAP, Christopher Janian of Vitruvius Co., one of the prospective developers, said that an evaluation of the building found significant water damage, making demolition the only viable option.

Any new development, regardless of what it was, won't be Martick's without Morris. "He was a very creative soul, very smart," said Rouse. "Just eccentric and a loner. And his paté was *incredibly* good."

9

Maison Marconi

OLD-FASHIONED AND TRADITIONAL
1920–2005

Maison Marconi was the kind of place that inspired loyalty from its guests. From well-heeled businessmen to legendary personalities, like H.L. Mencken, generations of Baltimoreans made Marconi's a part of their life stories.

Mencken famously called the restaurant "the Marconi" and preferred the broiled lamb chops, which, in his day, cost a whopping eighty-five cents. When he and his future wife, novelist Sara Haardt, lived on Cathedral Street, they were regular guests in Marconi's stately, brick West Saratoga Street building. Other famous guests included author Sinclair Lewis, publisher Alfred A. Knopf and actor and director Walter Huston—but Mencken is the one whose name is most frequently invoked by newspaper columnists reminiscing about the place.

Marconi's opened in 1920. Its founder and original chef, Fiorenzo Bo, was an immigrant from Turin, Italy, by way of London, where he cooked at Claridge's Hotel. Before settling in Baltimore, Bo lived in New York and Hampton Roads, Virginia. The restaurant's early history is a little murky, but according to a 1986 *Baltimore Sun* article by John Dorsey, Bo initially had a partner named Dominic. The pair briefly closed Marconi's and opened a very formal—and short-lived—restaurant on Cathedral Street. A 1929 notice in the *Sun* makes no mention of a "Dominic"—a man whose last name was lost to history—but it does say that a man named Eddie Ghislitta is no longer associated with Maison Marconi and that Fiorenzo Bo will retain control of the business.

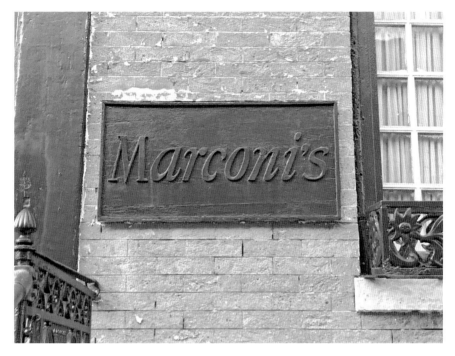

Maison Marconi sign. *Courtesy of Kit Pollard.*

Bo lived above the restaurant and was known for sitting in his window and watching people on the street. In September 1947, he fell out of the window and was no longer able to work after that. In his stead, Giacomo Cichero took over the kitchen. Chef Cichero remained the head chef until his death in the mid-1960s, when his protégé Antonio Sartori became head chef. Bo retained ownership of the restaurant until he died in 1954, at which point, longtime waiter and maître d' John C. Brooks took his place. Mr. Brooks, as he was known to both staff and patrons, started at Marconi's in 1926, as a twenty-year-old waiter.

In 1972, Mr. Brooks sold Marconi's to Louis Booke, a jeweler with a business across the street from the restaurant, and a car dealer named Harry Gladding. The sale was prompted by the building's placement on the market; Brooks didn't want to purchase it, so Booke and Gladding partnered to buy both the building and the business. Later, Booke, who bought the place because he liked the food and ate his lunches there, bought out Gladding. Throughout these changes in ownership, Brooks remained on staff, greeting customers five days a week, until he died in 1994. Like Marconi's, Brooks himself was such a Baltimore institution that his obituary was on the front page of the *Baltimore Sun*.

Despite the behind-the-scenes shifts in ownership, through the years, the Marconi's experience rarely changed. Fifty years after the restaurant's opening, Craig Claiborne wrote, in the *New York Times*: "A native Baltimorean remarked recently that nothing has changed at Maison Marconi in a hundred years...it is an old-fashioned, and in some ways, endearing place." The menu—and the staff preparing it—remained constant. By the time Chef Antonio Sartori retired in 1999, he had worked at Marconi's for forty-two years and had spent thirty-six of those years as the head chef. "He's the keeper of Marconi's traditions," wrote Carl Schoettler in a 1997 *Baltimore Sun* profile of Sartori. "[He] changes his menu about as often as Congress amends the Constitution." Schoettler described the chef as a "preservationist," noting that some of the menu's dishes had been around for longer than anyone could remember. "Marconi lore has it that 'lobster cardinal' appeared on the menu to honor Cardinal James Gibbons. He died in 1921."

Sartori was only the third chef in Marconi's history, and none of them had ever used printed recipes. Instead, they were passed down verbally and stored inside the chefs' heads. The food was a "unique blend of Italian, French and Maryland," wrote *Sun* restaurant critic John Dorsey in 1986. The temperature of the food was also paramount at Marconi's. The restaurant staff was careful to serve hot food on hot plates only, and cold on cold.

Native Baltimorean Betti Sheldon and her husband, John, were frequent Marconi's customers—as were their parents. Her regular order was the sole almondine and her husband's was the chopped salad, one of the restaurant's most famous dishes. "They would come and chop it right at the table," recalled Betti Sheldon. In a 2012 article, *Baltimore Sun* reporter Richard Gorelick got sentimental about the salad and its place in Baltimore's culinary pantheon. "Baltimore is one of the few cities where the chopped salad inspires memories of fine dining. For decades, a salad of iceberg lettuce, egg, tomato and anchovy, chopped tableside by a stiff-backed waiter, was one of the signature items at the old Maison Marconi," he wrote.

Another favorite of the Sheldons (and many others) was the chocolate sauce. "They'd bring a whole big sauceboat to the table and you could pour as much as you wanted," Sheldon said. In a 1988 *Baltimore Sun* article, restaurant critic Lynn Williams said, of the chocolate sundae: "This masterpiece, with its wealth of bittersweet chocolate sauce, is (like the restaurant itself) a legend in Baltimore gastronomy." Unfortunately, the chocolate sauce recipe seems to have died with the restaurant. The only real clue the restaurant gave the public was that it included Baker's unsweetened chocolate.

Former regulars recall the place as elegant and classic, with crystal chandeliers and traditional décor. Restaurant reviewers, on the other hand, who report without a cloud of happy nostalgia to cushion their memories, tend to be more critical. Lynn Williams's take on the space was somewhat jaded. She called Marconi's "a frumpy period piece, with linoleum underfoot and huge, dusty chandeliers above." She wasn't completely put off by that, though, writing, "It was great. The lack of pretension was a delight in itself, and eating among all this unchanged tradition—one of the veteran waiters looked as if he might have served Mencken—made the food even better."

In the late 1980s and 1990s, though Marconi's regulars remained loyal, the bloom started to come off the restaurant's rose just a bit. Articles that questioned the restaurant's place as a Baltimore classic appeared alongside those that praised the chocolate sauce. Reviews of the food were mixed and the charm of the place, to the outside critic, wasn't as consistent or readily apparent. In 1996, *Sun* writer Laura Rottenberg wondered: "Could our disappointing lunch and dinner there be explained away by saying we've moved on while Marconi's has remained constant?" At least, some writers mused, the prices were as old-fashioned as the food.

The Booke family didn't interfere much in the operations of the business until after Brooks's passing. In 1994, Ilene Booke, daughter of Louis, began to take a more active role in day-to-day operations. After Ilene took over, she spearheaded a revitalization of the restaurant that included replacing the old mural wallpaper with mint green paint and putting hardwood floors down in place of the old linoleum. These small changes were such a big deal that they made the newspaper. "For some people, that's tantamount to saying that the Sistine Chapel's ceiling got plastered over," wrote the *Sun's* Elizabeth Large. "But cooler heads will admit that it looks good." In the same article, Large quotes Marconi's maître d' Richard Ruben, who explained that every year, management tried to make a few improvements but that they didn't "want to do anything major. It might start a revolution." Marconi's, under the management of Ilene, also began accepting reservations for the first time and introduced valet parking.

Despite these changes, the restaurant still wasn't quite modern. In a 2000 article, *Sun* reporter Jacques Kelly called the restroom plumbing "antediluvian" but also praised the restaurant's "infectious way of balancing a formal—if idiosyncratic—way of delivering food with an understated manner of being gracious."

When Sartori retired in 1999, he was replaced by Keith Watson, and, in 2000, Peter Angelos bought the place from the Booke family, kicking off years of gossip and speculation about a possible relocation. When the news broke that Angelos was buying Marconi's, *Sun* writer Rob Hiaasen headed to the restaurant for lunch to catch the crowd's reaction, or lack thereof, as it turned out. "Yesterday at Marconi's, no one seemed broken up by the news of the sale or the pending move," he wrote. "Lunching ladies and salt-and-pepper-haired businessmen took their favorite tables. And, per custom, head waiter Ali Morsy knew everybody's name and drink order by heart. One imagines lunchtime on Wednesday had the same taste and feel of lunchtimes from long ago." Moving rumors were put to rest in 2004, when general manager Bassan Sara told the *Sun* that there were no plans to move. Just a year later, in July 2005, the restaurant closed.

Throughout Maison Marconi's lifespan, the world outside its doors had changed considerably, but the restaurant's place in Baltimore history has remained firm. "Marconi's is really Baltimore—it's a Baltimore icon," said Betti Sheldon. In 2002, the restaurant received a James Beard Foundation "America's Classics" award, but locals know that at its heart, Marconi's belongs to Baltimore.

10

Haussner's

A SPRAWLING MASTERPIECE
1926–1999

I t was time," said Francie Haussner George about the closing of her family's restaurant, Haussner's, in 1999. "It was old Baltimore." George and her husband, Stephen, who currently live in Millsboro, Delaware, spent decades working at the Highlandtown landmark that drew hundreds of thousands of diners over the years.

The history of Haussner's can be traced back to when George's father, German immigrant William Haussner, landed in Baltimore, where his brother Karl was living. William was a chef who had trained in various restaurants across Europe, and when he arrived in Baltimore, he went to work at Schellhase's, a German restaurant on Howard Street, where the "movers and shakers" lived at the time. Schellhase's has its own storied history as a hangout for journalist H.L. Mencken and his Saturday Night Club cronies, and luminaries like Sinclair Lewis, Henry Fonda and Lillian and Dorothy Gish, who would "feed their puppy samples of the restaurant's famed beefsteak tartare," according to a 1997 *Sun* story. By 1926, however, Haussner had opened his own place, a small eatery on Eastern Avenue in Highlandtown. In 1936, the restaurant moved across the street to a larger building, where it remained for decades.

The restaurant, which got a nod in a 2009 *Mad Men* episode, was celebrated for its old-school menu of German dishes and comfort food, elaborate Old Masters artworks, white-uniformed waitresses and the stag bar, which people still talk about, even though its all-male policy ended

Customers at Haussner's. *Courtesy of Baltimore Museum of Industry.*

in the 1970s. In a 1977 *Baltimore Sun* review, critic Elizabeth Large wrote, "Haussner's is, quite simply, an extraordinary restaurant, where everyone should have dinner at least once." She described her meal there as "a fine wiener schnitzel if you aren't feeling delicate," which was bolstered by two thick dumplings and rich sauerbraten gravy.

Haussner's dining room. *Courtesy of the Baltimore Museum of Industry.*

Tourists and locals kept Haussner's packed until its closure, and, although the restaurant was also frequented by celebrities, Francie George won't reveal names. She will only say that William Donald Schaefer, who served as Baltimore's mayor, state comptroller and governor, was often a guest. "We don't talk about our customers," she said. "People came in and sat at the same tables." Waitress Louise Barlow told *Baltimore* magazine, in May 2014, that she had worked at Haussner's for forty-three years. "Mr. Haussner was very fair, but he knew how he wanted things and catered to families," she told the publication. "I loved my work."

Fells Point resident Debbie Gerber remembers going to Haussner's as a child. "We would go on Mother's Day, Father's Day, all the holidays," she said. "My mother would dress us up, and we would wait for three hours, or so it seemed. It was first-come, first-serve, but the food was always good." Gerber is now married to Robert Gerber Jr., the man who bought Haussner's 825-pound, four-foot-wide ball of string for $8,000 when it was auctioned after the restaurant closed. "My husband loves Baltimore," she said. "He wanted it to stay in Baltimore." Francie explained the origins of the giant

Haussner's ball of string. *Courtesy of Gregory V. Haughey.*

ball: "My mother was a thrifty person, generous to a fault but thrifty," she said. When the restaurant's napkins were returned from the laundry, they were tied with string. Not wanting to waste the string, her mother, Frances Haussner, started rolling it into a ball that grew over the years.

Haussner's art collection—which included marble busts of Roman emperors and original paintings by van Dyck, Rembrandt and Bouguereau—was also sold at a 1999 auction by Sotheby's in New York for over $11 million. Today, former restaurateur Ted Julio, who owned Della Notte Ristorante in Little Italy, displays several of the busts in his Timonium home.

The Haussner's building was razed in 2016 to make way for an apartment building. Despite the restaurant's closure, generations of Baltimoreans still think fondly of its baked rabbit, grilled bratwurst and the famous strawberry pie squiggled with whipped cream. As diner Gene O'Conor wrote in a 1999 letter to the *Sun*: "Haussner's was a blessing for Baltimore."

11

Chesapeake Restaurant

AN ILLUSTRIOUS INSTITUTION
1933–1986

Philip Friedman's first job at his family's business, the Chesapeake Restaurant, was drying the silver when he was just a young teen. Later, he worked at the print shop on the premises, turning out menus after taking the streetcar from Forest Park High School to North Charles Street. His brother, Sidney Friedman—who was twenty years older than Philip—was in charge of the restaurant. Philip, who now lives in Pompano Beach, Florida, said that when Sidney joined the army, he was frantic about who would handle the menus. "I had been helping him," he said. "I told him, 'I can do that.'" Philip eventually went on to run the place.

The eatery was founded in 1918 by Morris Friedman—Sidney and Philip's father—as a small, storefront lunch counter with twenty-nine seats but, by 1933, had become one of Baltimore's top dining establishments.

At its peak, the Chesapeake drew powerbrokers, sports figures, celebrities and locals celebrating special occasions to its six dining rooms, which seated three hundred people on multiple floors. The restaurant's menu of charbroiled steaks, seafood dishes and stiff drinks, made with top-shelf brands like Tanqueray and Bacardi, complemented its clubby setting of dark wood, plush banquettes and white cloths on the tables. Even with an upscale ambiance, it was a comfortable place. "In spite of also being one of the city's truly expensive restaurants, the Chesapeake has a curious air of a family-owned, folksy, neighborhood establishment where everyone knows everyone else," Elizabeth Large wrote in the *Baltimore Sun* in 1973.

Chesapeake Restaurant owner Sidney Friedman. *Courtesy of the Baltimore Museum of Industry.*

The restaurant's former diners remember the place fondly, sharing memories on Facebook's "Baltimore Old Photos" page. Some of their quotes include: "One of my all-time favorite restaurants that had the best crab imperial," said Louis D. Jackson; "Lovely bar and restaurant," wrote Sharon Vukovan Larkin; "Absolutely fabulous," commented Alex Alexander; and "What a wonderful place. Will they ever [make] food like that again in Baltimore?" asked Eli Scar.

Sidney, along with his brothers, Phillip "Penny or Pinny" and Norman, and his sister, Ruth, later took over the operation when his father became ill, and they kept the restaurant going for decades. Other family members were involved, too, including Don Friedman, Philip's son, who would go on to open Gampy's in 1979 with his father. "I grew up at the Chesapeake," said Don, who now lives in Las Vegas. "At age eleven, I was printing menus."

Aside from the custom menus, former diner Ted Solomon of Butler remembers the embossed matchbooks that the restaurant would give to patrons who made reservations and the ten-cent check guests received to cover the cost of a phone call at the time when they made reservations. "It

Chesapeake Restaurant dining room. *Courtesy of Don Friedman.*

was quality service," Solomon said. "The Friedmans were nice people." Solomon also said he recalls the Chesapeake's claim that you could cut your steak with a fork or tear up the check. Beef dishes became popular at the Chesapeake after Sidney Friedman traveled to Chicago and learned about charcoal-broiled cooking. "None was being served on the East Coast," Philip Friedman said. In a 1973 *Sun* review, Large described a petite tenderloin steak she ordered as "cooked over charcoal" and "flavorful and rare," though she wasn't fond of the teriyaki sauce that came with it. The Chesapeake was also the first to serve Caesar salad east of the Mississippi, said Don Friedman. The salad became so popular that, when the kitchen couldn't get enough romaine lettuce, it used mixed greens and called it a Hollywood salad.

In 1976, Sidney retired, and Philip took over the business. The family was still trying to recover from a 1974 electrical fire that closed the restaurant for four months. It reopened on one floor but struggled before closing in 1983. Philip and Don Friedman bought the property again, and reopened the restaurant under the name, the Original Chesapeake Restaurant. The

Above: Chesapeake Restaurant menu from 1961. *Courtesy of Don Friedman.*

Left: Chesapeake Restaurant menu from 1941. *Courtesy of Don Friedman.*

Chesapeake Restaurant exterior. *Courtesy of the Baltimore Museum of Industry.*

Friedman family finally ended their run in 1986, but the good days aren't forgotten. "Almost everybody who was anybody in town came in," said Philip. He recalled the many times the manager of the New York Yankees, Casey Stengel, spent the evening regaling customers with stories and a time that Detroit Lions lineman Alex Karras came in with five fellow players and two coaches. He said they each ordered a lobster for two and twenty-two-ounce chateaubriands. Don said he also remembered a dinner visit by the vocal group the Temptations when he was in high school. "I heard the deepest voices," he said. "And there was [David Melvin English] and all [the band members] dressed in gold lamé outfits. Everybody came in."

The restaurant remained a Baltimore icon for more than fifty years. "We did very well," Philip said. "But times were changing."

12

Burke's Restaurant

KNOWN FOR POWER LUNCHES
1934–2010

The golden, three-inch-wide onion rings at Burke's Restaurant were so well-known in Baltimore that Oprah Winfrey, then a local reporter, asked about them at the restaurant when she was covering a news story for WJZ-TV. The kitchen obliged her with four carryout orders. "She was so happy," said Sandy Herrmann, the daughter of the restaurant's founders William A. Beery Jr. and Cricket Beery.

Herrmann, who is now a real estate agent living in Sparks, started working at her parents' restaurant when she was thirteen, cleaning tables and doing other tasks during the summer and on weekends. She eventually became a manager with her then-husband, Thomas Herrmann Sr., and her brother, Billy. "The three of us ran it for years," she said.

Burke's started as a working-man's bar in 1934 at the corner of Light and Lombard Streets. "Workers would come after their night shifts and throw back a shot and a beer," Sandy Herrmann said. "Later, my mother started serving food." The restaurant was named after a winning jockey, Johnny Burke, which played into its décor, said Tom Herrmann. The Burke family crest, which graced the walls of the restaurant and its exterior, was authentic. "We looked up the coat of arms in Ireland and made a copy," Herrmann said. "We used it as our coat of arms at the restaurant." Burke's Restaurant, sometimes called Burke's Café, eventually became known for its seafood and steaks. According to a 1976 advertisement, an eighteen-ounce strip sirloin steak cost $8.75 and a seafood platter with imperial crab, lobster lumps, fried shrimp, imperial

Left: Burke's Restaurant goblet. *Courtesy of Thomas Herrmann Sr.*

Below: Burke's bar. *Courtesy of Thomas Herrmann Sr.*

shrimp and scallops was sold for $6.75. A potent martini with three ounces of gin was available for just $1.00.

While Burke's was decorated in the spirit of a British pub, with a mahogany bar, wooden booths and tables, it also offered fare like sour beef with potato pancakes and German cabbage as well as club sandwiches, nachos and a crab melt on a muffin. A *Sun* reviewer wrote in 1985: "The eatery's appeal lies in its virtually unchanging menu and its mammoth beverage list (78 cocktails from $1.80 up)."

Sandy Herrmann remembers the stream of local and national celebrities who stopped by over the years. Many came in before performing at the nearby Morris A. Mechanic Theatre. When actor Vincent Price dined at Burke's, Herrmann said he loved the restaurant's scallops. "He actually went to the kitchen and asked how they were made." On another occasion, Robin Williams performed an impromptu standup routine in the upstairs comedy club, causing a lot of excitement among diners. Herrmann said she will never forget the time that the cast of *Oklahoma* burst out in song in the dining room during a visit. "Everyone went to Burke's at one time or another," she said. "We had regulars, and we had lines." Even the opening of Harborplace in 1980, with its glitzy new restaurants and stores, didn't affect the number of people who dined at Burke's. Lunchtime was particularly crowded with businesspeople who lingered over their meals.

Eventually, in 2010, the family decided to sell the restaurant, which was open twenty hours a day and served food until 1 a.m. Now, a Royal Farms store sits on the site. "Things changed," Herrmann said. "I loved the business. The clientele was great." On the "Baltimore Old Photos" Facebook page, group members fondly recalled Burke's: "How about those frosty mugs of beer with a big fat cheeseburger?" asked Dennis Blimline; "Best onion rings. Hot beef was also great," commented Annabelle Fangikis Setren; "I loved their crab imperial. One of my favorites," added Stephanie Porter. "I miss it so much."

13
Read's Drug Store

A LUNCH COUNTER SIT-IN
1934–1970s

With burgers, shakes and civil rights in mid-twentieth-century Baltimore, Read's Drug Store's lunch counter claimed a special place in history.

Read's was a chain of Baltimore drugstores founded in the nineteenth century by William Read. In 1899, the company was purchased by the Nattans family, who owned it until 1977, when the then one-hundred-store chain was purchased by Rite Aid. With stores scattered all over the city, Read's was part of the fabric of Baltimorean's lives for decades. "Run Right to Read's" was the store's slogan—and people did, both to purchase everyday items and to eat and drink at the stores' soda fountains.

Built in 1934, Read's four-story downtown store, located at the corner of Howard and Lexington Streets, was always busy and was a stellar example of the Art Deco architecture of the era. Two decades after it was built, the store made headlines for its role in the civil rights movement.

In January 1955, a group of seven students from Morgan State University, then called Morgan State, teamed up with the Congress on Racial Equality (CORE) to conduct a sit-in at Read's. The goal of the sit-in was to peacefully demand desegregation at the lunch counter. The twenty-minute protest was a success and led to a nearly immediate desegregation of lunch counters throughout the entire chain. On January 22, 1955, Arthur Nattans Sr., who was then the president of Read's, penned an announcement that ran in the *Baltimore AFRO-American* stating: "We will serve all customers throughout our entire stores, including the fountains, and this becomes effective immediately."

Read's Drug Store in 1965. *Courtesy of the Baltimore Museum of Industry.*

This announcement was an unequivocal victory for the civil rights movement and one that came five years before more nationally recognized sit-ins, such as the one at the Woolworth's counter in Greensboro, North Carolina.

Dr. Helena Hicks was one of the Morgan students who participated in the sit-in. In a 2012 interview with *City Paper* reporter Andrea Appleton, Dr. Hicks explained that, as a teen, she had been involved with the NAACP and was aware of ongoing protests related to segregation. After following *Brown v. Board of Education*, the 1954 Supreme Court decision that desegregated schools, Dr. Hicks said, "We were all very much aware of civil rights and that we could break down segregation barriers if we tried," she told the paper.

Before the sit-in, African Americans were allowed in some stores in the neighborhood, including the Berger cookie store, but they were not permitted to use the lunch counter at Read's. According to Hicks, "Read's didn't want you in there, period." On a chilly January morning, she and some friends decided to go into Read's, sit down and order a hot drink. "It wasn't planned. I mean, we didn't get together and say, 'We were going to do this,' and then proceed up there," she said. But, going in, they recognized that their action was one of protest and they believed they could win.

Dr. Hicks told *City Paper* that when she and her friends walked in, both Read's employees and other diners were shocked. Eventually, someone told them to leave. Though Hicks and her friends hadn't discussed it, they simply sat quietly. Only after the manager told them to leave "in a threatening way," did they get up and leave. "The press did pick up the Read's Drug Store sit-in—there were like three lines in the *Baltimore Sun*—and I'm glad they did because that was our only proof that it happened," Hicks recalled. That mention came on January 18, 1955, in a *Baltimore Sun* article about the state recommendation for integration. The article details Odell M. Smith's interview of William C. Rogers, the chairman of Governor McKeldin's interracial commission. In the article, they mention that the Sheraton-Belvedere Hotel had recently abolished discrimination in every part of the hotel, except for the bar due to liquor license requirements. In the article, Smith also says, "Likewise, Mr. Rogers disclosed, 37 stores in the Read drug chain are now serving both Negroes and whites." The success of lunch counter desegregation had a far-reaching impact.

During graduate school at Howard University, Hicks participated in additional sit-ins in restaurants and coffee shops in the area. "It was a continuous movement," she said. However, not everyplace was as quick to desegregate as Read's. "Read's was just the example of the very first that decided to cave in." In 2011, David Taft Terry, who was then the executive director of the Reginald F. Lewis Museum, told the *Baltimore Sun* that lunch counters were some of the few public spaces where black and white people "mingled" in public. "When you talk about shared public spaces, it was the lunch counters and the restaurants and the movie theaters. And it was the success of the sit-ins that opened the lunch counters."

Before and after the sit-in, lunch counters like Read's were popular places to eat. Everyone, from kids who took the streetcars from the outer edges of the city to office worker bees on their lunch breaks, frequented Read's for inexpensive hamburgers, grilled cheese sandwiches and thick chocolate milkshakes.

Read's occupies a role in the nostalgic memories of many Baltimoreans. In a 1991 *Baltimore Sun* article, Alice Steinbach reminisced about her time at a downtown YWCA summer camp, writing:

> At noon, we'd leave the Y and walk over to Read's Drugstore for lunch.… About a block away from Read's, you could start to smell the fragrance of roasted peanuts, the free ones being handed out by a man dressed in a peanut costume. We'd usually eat the hot, salted nuts sitting at the counter in Reads, waiting for our grilled cheese sandwiches and cherry Cokes.

Read's downtown location was the cause of some controversy in recent years, when developers wanted to raze the building to make way for a shopping district "superblock" development. Despite assurances from developers that any new building would honor and preserve the Read's legacy, there was significant pushback against redevelopment of the building. "The sit-in movement…begins in Baltimore. It begins with Morgan. It begins with Read's Drug Store. This is a national treasure," University of Maryland law professor Larry Gibson told the *Sun* in 2011. The case against demolishing Read's hinged on its historic importance, but some also noted that the building's Art Deco architecture was worth preserving.

The building, designed by local architects Smith and May, included intriguing design elements, like ships set into terra-cotta panels and "marine animals" on a metal rail on the dining balcony. The ships were a nod to the three-hundredth anniversary of the founding of Maryland, which coincided with the building's construction in 1934. The animals were included as a hint at the state's coastal location. The downtown location of Read's was the chain's most successful store, wrote Jacques Kelly in a 2009 *Sun* article, and it was housed in a "progressive, chic, modern building, trimmed with graceful windows and distinctive chromium signage."

Former location of Read's Drug Store in 2011. *Courtesy of Eli Pousson from the Baltimore Heritage organization.*

In August 2018, Baltimore's Commission for Historic and Architectural Preservation (CHAP) voted to create the Five and Dime Historic District in the West Baltimore downtown area where the former Read's building is located. In January 2018, the Baltimore Planning Commission voted to establish the district, and in March 2018, the city council voted in favor of the district. Part of the goal of establishment the historic was to make sure new developments honor the history of the region and to ensure that architectural elements are consistent with the neighborhood. The district is now part of a larger Market Center National Register Historic District, which includes Lexington Market and commercial buildings that housed nineteenth-century department stores, banks, theaters and restaurants.

The exact fate of the Read's building is still up in the air, but its lunch counter's position in history books—and in the memories of locals—is cemented.

14

Peerce's Plantation

GENTEEL SETTING IN THE COUNTRY
1937–2001

If you start chatting with Baltimoreans of a certain age, you'll find that more likely than not, they went to Peerce's Plantation a time or two in their younger days. Maybe they had dinner there before their junior prom, maybe they dropped in for a cocktail when they were a little older or maybe they dined there to celebrate a family event, with multiple generations at the table.

Despite the restaurant's name, Peerce's Plantation was never technically a plantation. The restaurant's roots go back to 1937, when William Peerce opened a dry goods store and gas station that served beer and wine in an old house overlooking the Loch Raven Reservoir. In 1941, during a farm equipment expo at the store, Marie Lake, a relation of Peerce's, sold some of her fried chicken to visitors. The chicken was a hit, and shortly thereafter, Marie and her husband, Duff, established Peerce's Plantation as a restaurant. Initially, the restaurant was a casual spot with outdoor seating, and it served dishes that included Marie's fried chicken, fried shrimp in a basket and soft-shell crabs. In 1963, the Lakes' twenty-one-year-old son, Peerce, took over the business and eventually transformed it into a more upscale establishment, where jackets and ties were required for men and lobster bisque and filet Chesapeake were popular dishes.

"It was like going out to the swankiest restaurant out in the woods," said John Shields, owner of Gertrude's at the Baltimore Museum of Art and a former Peerce's customer. With no air conditioning for years and a genteel country setting, Peerce's atmosphere was unlike anything else in the region.

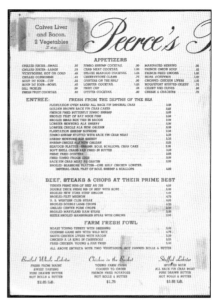

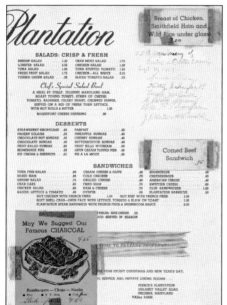

Peerce's Plantation menu from 1957. *Courtesy of the Rare Book Division of the New York Public Library. Retrieved from www.digitalcollections.nypl.org.*

"The feeling of it was very southern," remembers Brian Boston, a former Peerce's chef and current chef and owner of the Milton Inn. "Kind of New Orleans or Atlanta." Boston was fourteen years old when he started working at Peerce's in 1981. "It was a hustling, bustling kind of place," he recalled. At the time, Boston worked under executive chef Josef Gohring, but he also learned a lot from Edward Perry, the chef at Peerce's in the early days, when it was just a chicken stand:

> *Mr. Eddie Perry was my mentor when I started. Josef Gohring was the executive chef, but Mr. Perry was integral to the operation. He made the soup and sauces and was the backbone of the restaurant. I was his assistant. He'd send me off to get things so he could add stuff to the pot without me knowing. Within an hour of walking in the door, we'd have twelve or fifteen soups and sauces going.*

Boston worked at Peerce's until around 1984 and then came back in the mid-1990s to take over the kitchen. During the restaurant's early years, he said, on a typical Saturday night, it may have had six different private parties, plus a full house for regular dinner service. "Back then, we were doing enormous amounts of food," he said. "On any given Saturday, we were serving 400 to 800 people, and, on holidays, we were serving 1,200 to 1,500 people. It was a very busy place."

The kitchen made everything from scratch and broke down whole fish and legs of veal—and a lot of them. "We'd get twenty-five whole salmon in and butcher them, and they'd be gone the next day. I would pick two hundred pounds of crab meat to make crab cakes—that was a normal thing. I could spend my whole day just pounding veal, that's how it was," said Boston. The menu was classic American with a Chesapeake-southern twist. "[The dishes were] iconic Chesapeake, with all the things you'd expect," said Boston. "Oysters on the half shell, fried oysters, rockfish, big steaks." The crew, he said, was a blast. "It was a very tight-knit group of people working there, lots of neighborhood kids who went to school together. We had a lot of fun."

The crowd was a fun one, too. "All the movers and shakers were going to that place back then," said Boston. "The baseball players, the football players, that's where they went to eat. Everybody went to the Plantation for anniversary or celebratory events. Before prom, that used to be a really big thing." People would start coming in for dinner around 5:00 p.m., and, most nights, they'd still be coming through the doors at 11:00 p.m. "That was

Peerce's Plantation menu from 1973. *Courtesy of the Rare Book Division of the New York Public Library. Retrieved from www.digitalcollections.nypl.org.*

normal—from open to close. Every seat was taken, and people were waiting," he said. Boston remembers nights when the restaurant would lose electricity, but business would keep on humming. "Nobody left," he said. "We'd light candles in the kitchen—we had a whole system—and people were more than happy to stay. It made it more interesting. We'd switch to a menu we could handle on the instruments that were working. Those nights were exciting. The atmosphere of the place lent itself to something like that." John Shields remembers the bar at Peerce's as the ultimate sophisticated destination. "I loved the smell of the bar," he said. "In those days, it was cigarette smoke and whiskey, and it was the most grown-up, wonderful smell."

By the mid-1980s, Peerce's was the place to be. The 1988 *Baltimore Sun* dining guide acknowledged that its "genteel country-club setting" was home to "traditions that have stood for more than 40 years," but even so, the newspaper said it had gotten a bit "trendy." For a brief time, a couple of other Peerce's locations were opened. Peerce's Downtown, in Charles Center, was in business from 1980 to 1988, and in 1993, Lake opened Peerce's Gourmet, a carryout restaurant in Timonium that lasted for five years.

When Boston returned to Peerce's Plantation in the mid-1990s, the restaurant industry and local landscape had changed, so business was different, though Peerce's menu and atmosphere remained largely unchanged. Peerce's location was always off the beaten path for people who lived in or near the city, but in the early days, the restaurant got a fair amount of drive-by traffic. "Back then, people used to take Sunday drives," Boston said. "Loch Raven was closed off and back then you would have hundreds of people there, taking advantage." In later years, however, Sunday drives dwindled and, with them, the restaurant's audience. Plus, diners' interest in staid Chesapeake standards began to wane. Diners began to gravitate toward lighter, healthier and more varied choices, as opposed to the traditional, heavier Continental food Peerce's served. "Patrons and even reviewers today are always looking for the next best thing," said Boston.

In June 1999, *Baltimore Sun* restaurant critic Elizabeth Large reported on a disappointing meal at Peerce's. Boston was gone by then, and the restaurant had a new chef, but the menu still stuck with the classics. Unfortunately, Large found the food uneven and the service lacking. During that time, the business was already struggling. Peerce Lake had borrowed against the restaurant to finance his other ventures. In October 1999, a few months after Large's review and hours before a foreclosure auction was set to begin, the restaurant filed for bankruptcy, and Peerce Lake was able to retain ownership.

In 2000, Lake hired St. Michaels chef, Michael Rork, as a short-term consultant; he brought in the popular Towson chef Michael Gettier to take over the kitchen. Gettier made a few changes to the menu, but he didn't eliminate the old classics. As a result of his work, Peerce's garnered a welcome positive review from Large, who praised dishes like the pheasant sausage starter and whole roasted baby chicken served with bacon and leek. However, Large also warned, "Peerce's needs to rethink its basic concept if it wants to fill all those tables night after night." It was expensive, she noted, and still had the "special occasion" feel it had earned over decades, which was a more challenging label in 2000 than it had been thirty years before.

Gettier soon left Peerce's. In early 2001, Peerce's closed, and owner Peerce Lake put the building and adjoining property on the market. At that point, Peerce's Plantation had been in business for sixty-four years, and Lake's sons, Duff and Peerce Jr., and his daughter, Martha, had worked with him through everything. Lake told the *Baltimore Sun* that closing the restaurant was "a personal tragedy for my family and me."

In 2003, the restaurant reopened under new ownership; the business had been purchased at auction by Eric and Jackson Dott. The space received a makeover and so did the menu, though Chef Kevin Sonn retained many of the classics, like the filet Chesapeake and lobster thermidor. The reopening was a short-lived celebration, though; the restaurant closed again in 2006. After the restaurant's second closing, it was purchased by Joseph Bivona, who renovated and reopened the place. He renamed it the Grille at Peerce's, but it was put back on the market in 2014. But the Peerce's story isn't over yet; in 2019, it was reopened as an Indian restaurant run by Keir and Binda Singh, the brothers behind several esteemed restaurants, including the Ambassador Dining Room and Ananda.

Ultimately, Peerce's impact stretched far beyond the boundaries of its property. Throughout the city and surrounding areas, many waitstaff and kitchen teams can trace their roots back to Peerce's. Chef Josef Gohring went on to open a popular German restaurant, Josef's Country Inn in Fallston, and longtime manager Rudi Paul opened the acclaimed Rudy's 2900 in Finksburg. Boston continues to cook classics at the Milton Inn. "The filet Chesapeake comes from Peerce's," he said. "It's been on our menu [at the Milton Inn] for twenty-one years and a best seller for twenty-one years. It was a best seller at Peerce's—it's one of those tried-and-true things."

15

Velleggia's

ONE OF THE OLDEST ITALIAN RESTAURANTS
1937–2008

For residents of Little Italy and beyond, Velleggia's was more than just a restaurant. It was a gathering place and the heart of the community. In the days just after World War II, when Frank Velleggia Sr. was a little boy, he spent hours hanging around the customers in his parents' restaurant, listening to veterans, freshly back from the war, tell their stories. Velleggia's parents opened the restaurant in 1937; in the very early days, it was called Enrico's Friendly Tavern. "It was a small little place with a kitchen, a few tables," Velleggia recalled. His father, Enrico, was a stonemason by trade but an entertainer at heart. His mother, Maria ("Miss Mary" to locals), was the restaurant's culinary talent. "Miss Mary Velleggia was the true backbone of what we all grew to know Velleggia's as, which was a lovely, family, huge restaurant," said Giovanna Aquia-Blattermann, a longtime neighborhood resident and first-generation immigrant from Sicily, whose family owns the Little Italy establishments Café Gia and Pane e Vino.

"The place was very small, and, what happened was, a lot of my father's friends lived in this area, and, almost every weekend, they would come down, play cards, talk, argue," said Frank Sr. "As the years passed, we did a couple extensions, remodeling, and it got bigger." Aquia-Blatterman remembered:

> As it started to grow, [Miss Mary] began to buy around her to expand north and east. They started buying the properties if they went for sale, which then took them into High Street, so it became the whole corner. It was extremely big. It grew from Mr. Velleggia and his friends playing cards in the tavern to Miss Mary building an empire with her food.

That empire was truly a family affair.

After graduating from college in 1960, Frank Velleggia Sr. had plans to work in research science, but when his father fell ill, he was needed to help with the restaurant. "Once I got a taste of working at it on a full-time basis," Frank said, "it was hard to give it up. It was a lot of fun." Frank worked at the restaurant along with his brother, Naz, and several other family members. Naz was also the proprietor, starting in the 1970s, of Dici Naz Velleggia's in Towson, which he owned with Johnny Dee, who went on to open Johnny Dee's Lounge in Parkville. Dici Naz's evolved into Enrico's, named for the family patriarch, in 1993, but closed shortly thereafter.

Along with other midcentury Little Italy hot spots, like Maria's and Pisa's, Velleggia's was a frequent stop for the famous and powerful. Danny DeVito, Mae West and Joe DiMaggio all stopped at Velleggia's when they were in town. In the 1950s, Mayor Thomas D'Alesandro Jr. frequently held his staff meetings in Velleggia's. "And who would follow him in, but his youngest little daughter," recalled Frank Velleggia, Sr. That daughter, Nancy Pelosi, is now famous in her own right as a longtime member of the House of Representatives and Speaker of the House. Back then, however, "she was the shyest little thing," Velleggia said. He was a couple years ahead of her at St. Leo's, the neighborhood Catholic school.

Members of the Baltimore Colts were also frequent visitors; Velleggia remembers them calling from far-flung airports after away games, asking the family to keep the restaurant open late so that they could come in when they were back in town. The Velleggias always obliged. "They'd come and stay until all hours of the morning, rehashing their games," said Frank. Once a year, Velleggia's would host a polenta party for the team. "At that time, hardly anybody knew what polenta was," laughed Velleggia. "We would serve some wild game that friends of my father would bring—sausage and all—on top of the polenta and invite all the Colts, and they'd eat. Afterwards, they'd play poker. That went on for a good while."

In a 1971 article, *Baltimore Sun* restaurant critic John Dorsey called Velleggia's the "best known" of the Little Italy restaurants and noted that the menu was long and varied and that "the dining room, despite the fake kegs on the wall and the ersatz stained glass windows, is a pleasant room in which to dine." Dorsey praised a huge portion of homemade noodles, tossed with chicken livers and mushroom sauce, and a satisfying, if not terribly beautiful, veal saltimbocca entrée. The restaurant was "on the expensive side," he wrote, but it was an "enjoyable dinner."

In 1975, restaurant critic Elizabeth Large echoed Dorsey's criticisms of the dining room, calling it "downright ugly," but she was impressed with the food, particularly a combination platter including a homemade sausage. "The sausage is made fresh every day and simmered in white wine for this dish," wrote Large. "It shouldn't be missed."

In the early eighties, the restaurant underwent a massive renovation. "It's as if they threw away the old Velleggia's and brought in a completely new one to take its place," Large wrote in a 1983 review. The new space was shocking; it was "a sleek, glossy, contemporary-looking restaurant, oozing good taste," including a wine cellar with stained glass windows. Despite the physical changes, the kitchen was still turning out, "the dependable southern Italian cooking that 'Miss Mary' Velleggia began dishing out in the 1930s." Again, Large said she loved the sausage, and during her second visit, she also found the pretty pasta dish, paglia e fieno, "very alluring" and said, "Velleggia's knows how to fashion a proper saltimbocca."

Throughout the years, restaurant critics loved the service, even when the food wasn't quite perfect. In 1990, Mary Maushard called the service "superb" and said the restaurant catered especially well to kids, leaving her with "a good feeling, thanks to the warm atmosphere and friendly treatment."

Enrico Velleggia died in 1976, and Miss Mary passed away two decades later, in 1996. Both lived out their lives in an apartment above the restaurant they founded. Mary continued to run the kitchen until 1993, and even after she officially turned the reins over to her grandson Rick Velleggia, she visited the kitchen daily.

The Velleggia family was active outside the restaurant, too, advocating for the businesses and residents of Little Italy in a time when Baltimore City saw a number of changes. Frank Velleggia Sr. was president of the Little Italy Restaurant Association for years; during that time, he presided over numerous discussions with the city administration. "Some were pleasant, some were not," he said. The neighborhood unsuccessfully opposed the construction of Harborplace during Mayor William Donald Schaefer's administration, fearing that the restaurants included in the development would siphon business from Little Italy. "[But] it wasn't always a fight," Frank said. "We did quite a few combined efforts." Some of those united efforts included the restaurants banding together to host spaghetti parties at Rash Field, which attracted "tons of people" downtown even before Harborplace was built. Aquia-Blattermann remembers those days clearly. "Schaefer got his way, of course," she said. "For the first couple years, it was busy-busy; then, with all the restaurants in Harboplace, we lost our luster."

Frank Velleggia Sr. and Frank Velleggia Jr. at Casa di Pasta. *Courtesy of Kit Pollard.*

A few years after the opening of Harborplace, the development of Harbor East began, and with it came a change in traffic patterns. "While Velleggia's was the prime corner for sixty years to get into the neighborhood, it became no man's land," said Aquia-Blattermann. "So, that reversal hurt a lot of the business in north Little Italy. Those restaurants took a shellacking." A 2003 *Baltimore Sun* review by Elizabeth Large noted that, despite some lackluster food, Velleggia's was still bustling with parties and "the famous Little Italy service is alive and kicking…that wonderful combination of attentiveness and friendliness that doesn't step over the line to familiarity."

In 2005, real estate developer Terry Coffmann II purchased the restaurant from the Velleggia family with big plans to improve it. He kept the staff, slightly updated the menu and started planning for the restaurant's remodel, including a conversion of the building's upstairs apartments into additional dining rooms, increasing the capacity of the space. However, without the Velleggia family behind the restaurant—and Miss Mary's recipes in the kitchen—even loyal fans of the restaurant stopped coming. In 2008, Coffmann moved the restaurant to Water Street; two years later, he renamed it Supano's Prime Steakhouse Seafood & Pasta.

Meanwhile, back in Little Italy, the original building failed to sell at a foreclosure auction in 2009. Since then, the space briefly housed a Chinese buffet, Eagle House, and a sports bar called Boston's, which closed in October 2017, not even six months after it opened.

Though the Velleggia name no longer graces a Little Italy restaurant, the family's culinary legacy lives on at places like Liberatore's—family members behind that culinary empire worked at Velleggia's when they were younger—and Sabatino's. One of Sabatino's founders, Sabatino Luperino, worked as a chef at Velleggia's before venturing out on his own, in partnership with Joseph Canzani. The Velleggia legacy also persists in the freezer section of grocery stores, like Eddie's, which sell pastas created using old Velleggia family recipes. The pastas are produced by Casa di Pasta, a company Frank Velleggia Sr. opened about fifty years ago and which he still runs, along with his family, today. "I figured, my mother has some pretty good recipes," he said.

Generations of Baltimoreans agree.

16

Obrycki's Crab House

BIBS, MALLETS AND SPICY SEASONING
1944–2011

For decades, Obrycki's was *the* place to eat steamed crabs in Baltimore before it closed in 2011. Despite the restauraunt's closing, its name and quality seafood still survive at a restaurant and bar at Baltimore-Washington International Thurgood Marshall Airport. Diners, however, won't find the pounding of hot steamed crabs laden with black-pepper seasoning and the quaint Pratt Street surroundings that drew locals and out-of-towners looking for an authentic Baltimore experience.

The Obrycki's Crab House's original owners, Edward and Eleanor Obrycki, who are now deceased, opened their crab house in 1944 in upper Fells Point in a corner townhouse decorated with a Williamsburg flair. Inside, there was a wooden bar and a fireplace that created a welcoming atmosphere. Eleanor came up with the recipes, and Edward tended to the pots of crabs. In 1993, a *Baltimore Sun* reviewer wrote about a visit to the restaurant during its earlier days: "I never quite understood the reason for the wall sconces and the Colonial costumes, but couldn't fault the steamed crabs, fried stuffed shrimp or crab imperial. And people loved it." (Note: There was another Obrycki's restaurant at the time on Lombard Street, run by two of Edward's brothers and his brother-in-law. It was eventually sold and the building later burned down.)

In 1976, Richard and Rose Cernak bought the Pratt Street restaurant called "Olde Obrycki's" from Edward and Eleanor Obrycki, but they kept the Obrycki's name. Eventually, the restaurant moved to a larger location on Pratt Street, where it operated for decades. It was a family affair; the

Obrycki's exterior. *Courtesy of Obrycki's Restuarants.*

Cernaks' son, Rob Cernak, started working at the restaurant at age ten, when he wasn't in school. "We didn't have a babysitter then, so we went to the restaurant. I washed dishes, cleared tables. I worked every job," he said. Rob's sisters, Cheri and Cindy, and his brother, Rick, also worked at the restaurant, and they (minus Rick, who has gone on to other ventures) now own the airport eateries that are still called Obrycki's. They also run R&R Seafood Bar there, too, named after their parents, Richard and Rose. Rob's son, Rob Jr., is a general manager.

Rob Sr. has fond memories of his crab house days. "We had different celebrities visit the restaurant," he said. "The family misses meeting interesting people. At the airport locations, people come and go." The parade of power-hitters was never-ending when the seasonal restaurant was open from April to November. Danny DeVito, Neil Diamond, Bette Midler, Daniel Craig and Nicole Kidman were just a few of the famous names that stopped by for a taste of Maryland's favorite crustacean. Rob remembers a visit from actress Shirley MacLaine. He said she came in one night and saw one of the waitresses, Terry, who was "very loud, friendly [and] the life of the party," and the actress greeted her like they were best friends. That was the type of camaraderie people found at Obrycki's. Cheri Cernak recalls the athletes and coaches who visited the restaurant, admitting she isn't a big follower of sports and didn't always know who they were. In one instance, "a really big guy was buying carryout," she said. "I asked him if he had something to do with football," and he said he did. That man was the late Orlando Brown, a six-foot-seven-inch-tall, 360-pound lineman for the Baltimore Ravens.

The Cernaks also believed in having the right tools for their customers. They provided bibs, not typical at most local crab houses, and metal knives instead of plastic utensils to help diners separate the crabmeat from the shell more easily. Ted Solomon of Butler was a frequent diner at Obrycki's through the years and often visited twice a week. "I loved their crab soup. The fried clam strips were the best," he said. "I'd get the largest jumbo crabs, steamed spicy shrimp. I marvel at how much food I'd eat there." But he said it was the Cernak family who kept him coming back. "The magic of the place began with Rose and Richard. They were the heart and soul of the place," Solomon said. "They passed that on to their children."

The crab house also stood out for its seasoning. "I don't know where or how it started. It was part of it when my parents bought the restaurant," Rob Cernak said. "It was one of the things that made us unique. Not everybody loves it, but people who did, *loved* it." *Sun* restaurant reviewer Elizabeth Large commented on the mix in a 1982 review: "Obrycki's boasts its own secret spice mixture, and, for once, it isn't Old Bay," she wrote. "It's so fiery I might have it washed off next time. I did like it; I just found it hard to attack a crab when I was crying steadily."

After many years, the Cernak family decided to go in a different direction with their seafood business and shuttered the Pratt Street restaurant. "The reason for closing was quality of life," Rob Cernak said. "We were fortunate to change our business model and recapture our lives." Today, another restaurant, Angie's Seafood, has taken over the downtown spot, and is, once again, offering the familiar sound of cracking crabs.

17

The Eager House

EXPENSE ACCOUNTS AND CELEBRATIONS
1947–1986 AND 1993–1998

In its heyday, the Eager House in Mount Vernon was a special occasion destination, drawing well-heeled diners with its offerings of charcoal-cooked steaks, Chesapeake Bay seafood and an impressive wine list. Its owner, Bill Tutton, was the restaurant's gregarious, genial host, who playfully told young diners that the restaurant's Crow's Nest dining room, which was decked out in a nautical style, was a boat. The waitresses even wore sailor suits to carry out the theme.

Tutton opened the Eager House in 1947 in a turn-of-the-century building that once housed his father's lunchroom, and he transformed it into a swanky, upscale restaurant. Besides the seafaring theme, the decor also included "black imitation leather with studs in it, marbleized mirrors, and lots of red all over everything," wrote *Baltimore Sun* restaurant critic John Dorsey in 1972. In the same article, Dorsey added: "We had a splendid time at the Eager House. It was horribly expensive, yes, but less than certain restaurants around town that do less to justify their prices.…The food and service were exceptionally good for a typical American restaurant."

Buzz Beler, the owner of the Prime Rib restaurants, including one in Baltimore, said in Tutton's 2004 *Sun* obituary: "The Eager House was always a big-time place and was the best in town. It was the place to be seen." Beler also described a house specialty, the oyster roast Eager House, "which were oysters on the half shell, topped with backfin crab," and mentioned a "tank with lobsters that could be prepared nine ways." A 1961 newspaper ad promoted the Eager House's Charcoal Room, where "steaks and chops hiss

Eager House dining room. *Courtesy of the Baltimore Museum of Industry.*

and sizzle over glowing embers" and its Antique Motor Bar, which had an antique car on display amid "white ornamental-iron glass-top tables, leather upholstered lounges, and service reminiscent of days gone by."

Along with the Eager House, Tutton also operated the neighboring Gaslamp Club, a private dinner club with "scantily attired waitresses," according to the *Sun*. In later years, business declined at the Eager House, and Tutton sold the restaurant and the Gaslamp Club in 1976. After that, the restaurant became a revolving door of proprietors for the next twenty years. Even *Sun* restaurant critic Elizabeth Large wrote in a 1982 review: "I've lost count of how many times the establishment has reopened under new names and new owners."

After the original Eager House closed, the restaurant at 15 W. Eager St. quickly reopened following renovations the same year. Large described the restaurant as "livelier and busier than it used to be, particularly in the evening. It's still Baltimore's expense-account restaurant par excellence." After five years, that Eager House closed, and Morgan's opened in its place before it also closed. Soon, another restaurant opened with the name

The Eager House building in 2019. *Courtesy of Gregory V. Haughey.*

Eager House, and its menu featured "steak and seafood with a Continental accent," Large wrote. By 1982, with new owners, the Eager House was able to maintain its glamorous image, with a piano player and, according to Large, "good American food with a Spanish slant." However, that restaurant also eventually closed.

In 1993, businessman Ernest L. Murphy bought the property, which, at that point, had been shuttered for seven years. He spent almost $1 million on renovations with the hopes of restoring the Eager House to its former glory. "I was looking for a new business opportunity and, for some reason, thought a restaurant was a good choice," said Murphy, owner of Hospitality Development Company III. "I've always been interested in historic properties." He opened the restaurant with an American fine-dining menu prepared by executive chef Christopher Golder. Unfortunately, the timing was bad economically for the restaurant business, Murphy said. "I got frustrated one evening and just closed it," he said. The property was for sale again in 1998.

The space soon became Paloma's at Eager House, a bar-restaurant with game rooms. After that, it became Eden's Lounge, a nightclub that folded in 2013. The building was eventually sold again, and at the time of this book's publication, a developer was planning to construct a multi-use building on that site and adjoining properties.

To this day, diners recall the good years at the Eager House on Facebook's "Baltimore Old Photos" page with comments like: "Went there several times for special-occasion dinners in the 1970s. Always delicious" and "Loved the atmosphere, service, food, and especially the baked Alaska! Good memories!"

18
Jimmy Wu's New China Inn

CHINESE FOOD TO SAVOR
1948–1983

According to an old tale, one night, in 1941, Jimmy Wu was dining alone in the China Inn, where he had just become a partial owner. After eating his meal, he opened a fortune cookie to find a promise: "You will have a long and successful life in Baltimore's Chinese restaurant business. And you will be thought of fondly for it." This story, which was shared by *Baltimore Sun* reporter and local historian Gilbert Sandler, might be too perfect to be true, but even if it's nothing more than a tale once told by an aging restaurateur, it's appropriate.

Jimmy Wu—whose full name was James Lem Fong Wu—was a Cantonese immigrant who moved to the United States when he was fourteen. Upon settling in Baltimore, Wu's father worked in restaurant kitchens before opening an import shop on Mulberry Street in the city's original Chinatown neighborhood.

Wu's first foray into the restaurant business was in Chinatown proper— the area around Park Avenue and Mulberry Street. After graduating from City College high school in 1933, Wu began waiting tables at the China Inn, and, in the early 1940s, he became a partner in that establishment. Along the way, he got married to a woman named Jean, and, together, they had four children. In 1948, Wu opened a place of his own—the New China Inn—a few blocks to the north of the original China Inn.

Located on North Charles Street near Twenty-Fifth Street, Jimmy Wu's restaurant occupied several row houses. Inside, it had multiple dining rooms; some were formal and slightly over-the-top, and some were less so. The

Jimmy Wu's "The New China Inn" postcard. *Courtesy of Kit Pollard.*

dining rooms had names like "Forbidden Quarters" and "Longevity Room," and the decor included Chinese lanterns, scrolls and a green-and-red color scheme. Compared to other Chinese restaurants around town, Jimmy Wu's was considered nicer, a place where customers didn't feel out of place if they dressed up to dine. Of course, that was back when "a Chinese restaurant was considered swanky if the waiters didn't wash down the Formica tabletops with the leftover tea," *Baltimore Sun* restaurant critic Elizabeth Large mused in a 2003 column.

The drinks at Jimmy Wu's were fun and tropical—the cocktail menu was pages and pages long—and if the food wasn't always adventurous or perfectly prepared, at least it was predictable and comforting. "That was one of the first places I ate Chinese food," recalled native Baltimorean Meg Fairfax Fielding. "It was so old school Chinese. I'm sure it was really Americanized Chinese food, and I'm sure no Chinese person would recognize it now!" The service at the New China Inn was generally known as good, and Jimmy Wu himself was a standout. Even in the last days of the restaurant, he was a presence in the dining room, making his way from table to table, greeting guests.

Jimmy Wu's was also the first Chinese restaurant to be reviewed in the *Baltimore Sun.* "This may not be the best Chinese restaurant," wrote critic John Dorsey, "but it's certainly the most popular." Everybody may have gone to Jimmy Wu's, but that doesn't mean that it was taken seriously in the same way that American or French restaurants of the day were. That review didn't run until 1971, over twenty years after the restaurant opened. In terms of food, Dorsey's feedback was mixed. He said he liked the shrimp toast ("delicate and delightful") and the egg rolls ("not too heavy") but called the spareribs "inferior" and was disappointed to discover that they were pork ribs, not beef. He got some pushback, though, from Jimmy Wu's fans. In the weeks after the review ran, the "Letters to the Editor" section was packed with people offering their own, more positive, take on the New China Inn's food (and their less than positive thoughts about Dorsey's expertise). "What kind of expert is your critic? A gourmet he is not," wrote Elisabeth R. Gladding, a Baltimorean who described herself as an "enthusiastic customer of the China Inn since its founding."

The restaurant ran frequent ads in the *Sun* that would raise eyebrows in modern times. Today, some of them would be perceived as outright racist; for example, a 1949 ad for Christmas dinner including the words, "Jimmy Wu says, 'Melly Klistmas.'" Similar jokes were carried into the restaurant as well. A 1975 *Sun* restaurant review mentions that one of the bartenders was called "Won Long Pour" and that language like "Velly Sorry" could be seen on carry-out menus. Even then, critic Elizabeth Large called the angle "irritating humor." Wu leaned into Asian stereotypes in his advertising, but he also touted the power of food to unite and bridge cultural gaps. "One language that anyone can understand is the universal language of good food," said a 1947 *Sun* advertisement. Another ad from 1948 said, "From Shanghai to Chicago, from Tokio to Taneytown—Jimmy Wu's New China Inn in Baltimore is famous for fine food."

Later, Wu opened carry-out shops on East Cold Spring Lane and in Cockeysville. He was also an active member of the local Chinese community: he opened a Chinese language school, sponsored immigrants and volunteered with the Chinese Benevolent Association.

Given the tenure of Jimmy Wu's—it was open for nearly half a century—it's not a surprise that diners' tastes changed while it was in business. The New China Inn was innovative and educational in the 1940s, but, eventually, Baltimoreans grew savvier. In her 1975 review, Elizabeth Large wrote, "People are more sophisticated about Oriental food these days, but Jimmy Wu's still does very well selling egg rolls and sweet and sour pork and chicken chow mein. Why change a good thing?" Despite this good review, by the early 1980s, the Cantonese style of Chinese cooking that Jimmy Wu's specialized in was on its way out, in favor of the more modern, spicier Szechuan style. The evolution in cuisine was part of a larger cultural shift, as new Chinese immigrants, many from the area around Peking, came to the United States starting in the 1970s after President Nixon opened diplomatic relations with China. These immigrants brought their cuisine with them and offered an alternative to the milder and more established Cantonese style of cooking.

Initially, Jimmy Wu's resisted the change, standing by the superiority of Cantonese cuisine. Eventually, though, Wu caved to public opinion. In the early 1980s, he hired a Szechuan chef, Chen Kwan, and radically updated the menu. Even then, the restaurant took its conservative audience into account. "Jimmy Wu's is a good place to start for those who want to be introduced gently to Szechuan food, who are nervous about dishes that contain whole hot peppers or who don't think they'd like food flavored primarily with scallions, garlic, ginger and hot pepper flakes in oil," wrote Large in a *Baltimore Sun* review that was published shortly after the new chef came to town. During that visit, Large noted that dining at the New China Inn "[was] a visit to the past, when Chinese restaurants were exotic, just slightly mysterious and gloriously gaudy with a touch of seediness." At the same time, she acknowledged that Jimmy Wu's had a reputation for serving "Americanized" cooking."

Jimmy Wu's new focus on Szechuan cuisine didn't last long. In 1983, the restaurant closed and a new concept, Szechuan Gourmet, opened in its space. At the time, Large called this change, "typical of the city's move away from old-fashioned food." Jimmy Wu had a small share in Szechuan Gourmet, which was primarily owned by Paul Chao, but he had no major role in operations. For several years, Wu had suffered from health problems, and when he announced the closing of his restaurant, he explained that due to his age, he simply couldn't keep up with the work anymore. Unfortunately, he didn't have much of an opportunity to enjoy his retirement; he died in early 1984.

Wu recognized his own impact, though. In 1982, he told the *Baltimore Sun*, "Life has been rewarding, has been interesting to me. And Baltimore, particularly, has been good to me. And I hope, in a way, I have contributed something to Baltimore all these years, in the way of serving people, introducing them to Chinese food, and helping to make Chinese food in the city of Baltimore."

19

Harvey House

NAMED AFTER AN INVISIBLE RABBIT
1951–1993

Harvey House in Mount Vernon was a happening place in its day. "It's almost like a club," said owner Lou Baumel to the *Baltimore Sun* in 1992. "People feel like they belong here. People like it because their name is known and recognized." At that time, the restaurant had been in business for forty years and was known for its lively clientele, piano bar and varied menu that included prime rib, crab cakes, shrimp fra diavolo and potato pancakes with applesauce. Each meal started with an appetizer of dainty chicken-liver canapés.

"Everything was real, made from scratch," said Diane Feffer Neas, a local restaurant consultant who dined there. "They had the best chicken liver ever. They put honey in the chicken liver. I also liked the chicken in the pot." Pumpernickel rolls with coarse salt and caraway seeds always graced the tables while diners waved to friends from across the dining room or went table-hopping to greet them in person. "On a Saturday night, eating at the Harvey House is like being at a large, noisy, crowded party," *Sun* restaurant reviewer Elizabeth Large wrote in 1979. Shirley Weiner, the daughter of the late Lou Baumel, remembers the crowds. "We saw the same people every week," she said. "It was like family."

The restaurant's exterior was an appropriate introduction to the restaurant's atmosphere, with its lavender façade and large neon rabbit on the door. Inside, diners were treated to orange and yellow brick walls, green plants, paintings, knickknacks, including cut glass and decorative plates, that lined shelves and curio cabinets that were collected by

Harvey House postcard. *Courtesy of Suzanne Loudermilk*

Weiner's mother, Rose. But it was the cottontail mascot that got everyone's attention at 920 North Charles Street at a time when the Baltimore thoroughfare was bustling with shops and other dining establishments. When Baumel opened the restaurant in 1951 with Rose, he named it after the six-foot-tall invisible bunny in the play *Harvey* and after one of his sons, who was named Harvey. The name can also be traced back to the first Harvey House restaurants that were developed in the West in the 1870s to feed railroad passengers and to the Harvey Girls, who served as waitresses there. "My dad loved that name," Weiner said. "It was the perfect fit for him."

Lou Baumel learned to cook aboard ships while serving as a merchant marine, according to his 1996 obituary in the *Sun*. When he returned to Baltimore, he worked in the kitchen of the Club Charles, a popular supper club in the 1940s and 1950s that drew entertainers like Jackie Gleason, Tony Bennett and Dean Martin and Jerry Lewis before he opened the Harvey House, where he would hold court for decades. "People would call my mom Miss Rose," Weiner said. "My dad was the greeter." After opening his own restaurant, Lou Baumel often traveled to Europe to take wine courses and brought back recipes he discovered there, like the Caesar salad that was made tableside and French onion soup with a crouton and melted cheese on top.

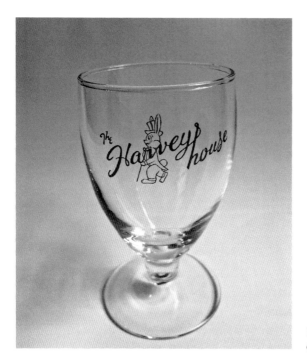

Harvey House glass. *Courtesy of Brennen Jensen.*

The Baumels eventually left their Pikesville home in the suburbs and moved atop the restaurant. "There was a love affair between my parents and the city," said Weiner, who, at the time, called her father the "mayor of Charles Street." "They spent the last years of their life there." Weiner's brother, Barry Baumel, also worked in the Harvey House, starting when he was seven or eight years old, washing dishes. In high school, he was a busboy and waiter, and after college, he said, "I took on many jobs. Eventually, [the restaurant] fell into my hands many years later."

In the 1950s and 1960s, the three-martini lunch was still in vogue, Baumel said, but the world was evolving. "People stopped drinking as much," he said. "People moved away. It had its time."

After many successful years, the Harvey House closed in 1993. "It was very homey," Weiner said. "It was a beloved restaurant."

20

Pimlico Hotel

WHERE THE FAMOUS WOULD GO
1951–1991

The story of the Pimlico Hotel restaurant is one that is dramatic and filled with late nights, long menus and boldfaced names. But underneath the glitz and glamour, it's also a tale about the changing landscape of Baltimore.

During its most famous years, the Pimlico Hotel was strictly a restaurant, without any rooms for rent, but originally, it *was* a hotel. The Pimlico was built in 1875 in the infield of the Pimlico Race Course as a place for people involved with racing to stay. Later, it was moved to the corner of Park Heights and Hayward Avenues, where it continued to operate as a hotel— one with a somewhat seedy reputation. It was raided multiple times during Prohibition, and, in the 1930s, it was a barbershop and bar where bets were taken. In 1950, the building's fortunes took a turn for the better, when Leon Shavitz and Nathan Herr, business partners who owned a North Avenue deli called Nate's and Leon's, bought it and transformed the ground floor into a swanky restaurant. "The Pimlico was the first upscale neighborhood restaurant that existed," said Charles Levine. Levine, who now co-owns Citron in Quarry Lake with his wife, Susan, started working in the kitchen at the Pimlico when he was young. Glam as it was, the Pimlico was also, at its core, a family business. After several years, Leon Shavitz bought Herr out of the restaurant. In 1959, Shavitz's sons-in-law, Lenny Kaplan (married to Gail) and Alfred Davis (married to Reta), both got involved in the business. Charles Levine fits into this story, too: he is Davis's nephew.

The restaurant drew a starry crowd, including celebrities who came to town for shows or for the Preakness. "I served Arnold Schwarzenegger," remembered Levine. "They all came—Jack Benny, Johnny Carson. People came to Baltimore and went to the Pimlico." The walls of the restaurant were covered with signed portraits of famous faces, from Mitzi Gaynor to Brooks Robinson and Angela Lansbury. But it wasn't just the famous who flocked there. "People [went] there, it was their hangout, their club," said Levine. "There weren't a lot of places to go, and in those days, people wanted to go where other people were." On a typical Thanksgiving or Mother's Day, the restaurant would serve a thousand people, said, Levine. "We'd have cars backed up for six blocks."

The restaurant's popularity was a generally accepted fact. *Baltimore Sun* restaurant critic Elizabeth Large opened a 1974 review with, "It hardly seems worth writing about the Pimlico Hotel. Surely everyone in Baltimore must not only know about it, but eat there." There were never reservations available—you had to know somebody to get in, and once you got there, the tables were close together. "You could never get a seat in the bar," said Levine. People didn't seem to mind, however. "It was happy, wonderful, delicious. Who wouldn't want to be sitting next to a celebrity? Who wouldn't want to go into the bar and meet people?" According to Levine, there was also an intrigue and a sort of wildness to the restaurant; regulars would turn up with their wives one night and their mistresses the next. "Whatever happened at the Pimlico stayed at the Pimlico," he said. "And a lot happened."

Every Thursday night, the restaurant hosted live music and Mondays were talent nights hosted by Trucky Halpren, a local celebrity in his own right. "It was funny and dirty," said Levine. "It would never exist in today's world. It just couldn't."

When Shavitz died in 1977, Alfred Davis, Lenny Kaplan and another local restaurateur, Hersh Pachino (though his involvement was short-lived), took over the operations of the restaurant. Even in Shavitz's absence, the Pimlico remained the place to be.

While the crowds came to be seen, both before and after Shavitz's passing, they also came for the food. "We had really delicious food," said Levine. "The meat was prime and we cut it ourselves. The salad was bountiful. Big shrimp cocktail, jumbo lump crab meat. It was fabulous food and everything was specialized for you." The menu at the Pimlico was famously long and varied. "[The restaurant] had a huge menu," remembered longtime Baltimorean Merle Porter, who dined at the restaurant when she was young. "You could get seafood, salads, everything." The menu also stretched beyond American

Frank Sinatra and Hersh Pachino at the Pimlico Hotel. *Courtesy of Hersh Pachino.*

borders. "How many restaurants offer an enormous variety of American beef and seafood and French-influenced dishes—and just as many Cantonese ones?" asked Elizabeth Large in a 1979 *Baltimore Sun* review. "Some say it has the best Cantonese food in town."

Possibly the most iconic dish on the menu was the Coffey salad, named after longtime, beloved waitress Claudia Coffey. In 1983, the *Baltimore Sun* called the then seventy-year-old Coffey the "Grande Dame" of waitressing. At that point, she'd been working at the Pimlico for nearly a quarter of a century and had been waitressing for over fifty years altogether. She came up with the salad and prepared it tableside for guests. "It was a lot of cheese, a lot of garlic and was so fresh," said Levine. Plus, like everything else at the Pimlico, it would be customized. "If you came in, she would know if you didn't want a lot of tomatoes," he said.

The inside of the restaurant was like a Rube Goldberg machine in the way it was laid out, according to Levine, with twists and turns and odd pathways to manage when shuttling food between the kitchen and dining room. "But the Napoleon never fell and the éclair never sweat," said

Levine. Meals may not have been quick to arrive, Levine remembered—but that didn't matter. "Sometimes tickets in the kitchen were ridiculously long, but people didn't care. They were at the Pimlico and that's where they wanted to be," he said.

In the 1970s, crime was on the rise in the neighborhood around the restaurant, and even a place like the Pimlico Hotel, with its strong following, wasn't immune to that impact. "As the neighborhood changed and things got a little more dangerous, they put a fence up around the parking lot and valeted," said Porter. "But still people came." But that business did not last forever. In 1981, the owners were taking steps to relocate outside of the city, citing a "concern for their customers well-being in the neighborhood," according to a *Baltimore Sun* article. The actual move took a few more years: the old restaurant closed in February 1984 and reopened later that year in a new Pikesville location. "When they moved, the clientele went with them," said Porter. The original location was demolished in 1985 to make way for a McDonald's. Today, a self-storage facility stands on that corner.

"The old Pimlico was a belated victim of suburban flight, of changing racial and economic patterns in Northwest Baltimore," wrote the *Sun's* Michael Olesker in 1985. "It was an oasis of culinary sumptuousness and schmoozy elegance that somehow lingered…long past a time any wise-guy tout would have wagered it would last."

Within the company there were struggles, too, born out of working with family. A few years after the move, in 1987, the Davises bought the Kaplans out of the business. The Kaplans left to open Classic Catering and, eventually, to start the Polo Grill. "We had different ideas about how or what the direction of the Pimlico would be," Lenny Kaplan told the *Sun* in 1990.

In the 1987 dining guide, *Baltimore Sun* writer Janice Baker described the new restaurant's ambiance as "ease and comfort." It was one part elegant—"white linen, immaculate glass and mirrors, dressy guests"—and one part easy informality, with friendly waitresses and "an enormous menu." The new location was a hit for a few years, but its success didn't endure. The Pimlico Hotel closed its doors in November 1991. On the last night of business, waitress Claudia Coffey was distraught, as were many of her longtime customers. "This is really heartbreaking," she told the *Sun*. That evening, almost six hundred people came to reminisce, pay their respects and dine at the Pimlico one last time.

Today, the Pimlico Hotel's Pikesville location is a Ruth's Chris Steakhouse, but reminders of the old Pimlico days pop up here and there on menus throughout the city. At Citron, the Pimlico cake, a chocolate cake layered with custard, makes appearances on the menu. As for Charles Levine, the lessons about relationships and hard work that he learned in his early days at the Pimlico have influenced how he does business today. "It was crazy—it was so busy," he said. "There was so much to learn. So much action."

21

Danny's

UPSCALE AND FRENCH
1961–1991

When noted *New York Times* restaurant critic Craig Claiborne praised Danny's in a 1977 article, Baltimoreans paid attention—not that they didn't already know that the renowned restaurant was worthy of favorable comments. Claiborne wrote about his visit: "I had sampled Danny's crab cakes, and it was a devastatingly gratifying, unforgettable experience that could be likened to the first taste of a wild raspberry or homemade peach ice cream. There was not a disappointment the second time around." But he also reminded readers that Danny's wasn't a crab house: "It has a French kitchen and takes itself seriously as such," he said.

Danny's was the brainchild of Danny Dickman, a hands-on, front-of-the-house host, who founded the Mount Vernon restaurant in 1961. He wanted to replicate some of the top French restaurants he had visited in New York, according to his 1993 obituary in the *Baltimore Sun*. His plan succeeded, with his restaurant eventually receiving multiple awards, including a four-star rating in the *Mobil Travel Guide* and a nod for distinctive dining in *Holiday* magazine. Diane Feffer Neas, a local restaurant consultant, told the *Sun* in 1991: "Culinarily speaking, [Danny Dickman] put Baltimore on the map. For years and years and years, Danny's was *the* restaurant in Baltimore."

Danny Dickman's wife, Beatrice, and their son Stuart were also prominent presences in the restaurant, showing diners to their seats or preparing some of Danny's tableside dishes, like steak Diane and Caesar salad. Ted Solomon of Butler recalled many visits to Danny's. "It was very

Danny's exterior. *Courtesy of the Baltimore Museum of Industry.*

family-oriented with quality service and had a nice atmosphere," he said. "[The Dickmans] were nice people."

Before the restaurant's fancy Continental dishes would arrive at diners' tables, the waitstaff served kosher pickles and large, hot popovers to tease diners' appetites. Then, the main event began. With a dedication to fresh foods, Dickman flew in items like Dover sole, Scotch salmon and petits pois

Danny's dining room. *Courtesy of the Baltimore Museum of Industry.*

from France. He also made regular trips to local markets for fresh ingredients. His efforts paid off. In a 1973 *Sun* review, Elizabeth Large enthusiastically wrote about the restaurant's "beef en croute Wellington": "It would make angels weep. The chef begins with at least an inch and a half of prime filet. He covers it with a thin layer of paté and wraps it in puff pastry, incredibly light and crisp and unbelievably rich." In her article, Large also described the decor in the restaurant's Escoffier Room, complete with a portrait of the French chef, Georges Escoffier, as "subdued and slightly gaudy at the same time, with crystal chandeliers, red plush and gilt....The nicest part of the surroundings is the food."

Local reviewers also praised the restaurant's chocolate-chip cookies and mints that were served after sumptuous desserts, like baked Alaska and cherries jubilee. An extensive wine list, with some bottles costing over $1,000, was also available. "Dinner at Danny's is not an inexpensive outing, but well worth the money for a special occasion," wrote food editor Mary Maushard in the *Evening Sun* in 1990. "Not only were the food and service virtually incomparable, but we were also made to feel comfortable."

The Dickmans knew about hospitality and service, but after thirty years in business, Danny Dickman was ready to retire and sold the restaurant in 1991 to his son and daughter-in-law. The two eventually became involved in a bitter divorce, and Danny's closed that year.

Baltimoreans still recall Danny's happy times. Lydell Mitchell, a former Baltimore Colts running back, told the *Sun* in 2016: "I remember Danny himself would come out and greet you…The restaurant not only had his name, but it had his stamp on it. He just had a ray in him that was filled with life. I just loved being in his company."

22

Bernie Lee's Penn Hotel

A SOCIAL AND POLITICAL CLUB
1967–1974

I f you mention Bernie Lee's Penn Hotel in Towson, old-timers will tell you how it was a hub for Baltimore County lawyers and politicians who were plotting court cases and election runs. But that was only part of the restaurant's story before its demise in the 1970s. Generations gathered there for food, fun and festivities.

Despite its name, the Penn wasn't a hotel but a restaurant during its heyday from the late 1950s to mid-1970s. It served traditional American fare with a Maryland spin (crab with Smithfield ham, terrapin soup and fried chicken) in its dining rooms and stiff drinks in the Quill Club and Stag Bar on the premises. A devoted patron at the time, the now deceased Baltimore County circuit judge, John Grason Turnbull, particularly took note of the watering hole's stellar mint julep, according to news reports.

"Bernie Lee" was attached to the restaurant's title after Bernard J. Lee Jr., who had managed the restaurant for almost ten years, purchased the property in 1967. "He was a terrific guy," said Bill Hahn, a longtime Towson attorney who started going to the Penn Hotel when he was a student at Loyola Blakefield high school in Towson and eventually held his bachelor party there in 1968. "He was the greeter at the door." Hahn remembers digging into many of the restaurant's great steaks, sandwiches and crab cakes over the years. After Lee passed away in 1972, "it became a different place," he said.

Bernie Lee's daughter, Maureen Tipton, who lives in Perry Hall, spent much of her time at the Penn Hotel while growing up—she bussed tables,

Bernie Lee, owner of Bernie Lee's Penn Hotel. *Courtesy of the Baltimore Museum of Industry.*

worked in the kitchen and helped with the restaurant's catering after her school day ended at Towson High School. "It was a fun life," she said. "It was a happy place."

In addition to its attorney clientele, Tipton said the restaurant drew local sports figures, including Orioles third baseman Brooks Robinson and Baltimore Colts quarterback Johnny Unitas, who liked to hobnob with her father. "He was Mr. Personality," Tipton said. "He was everybody's friend." Tipton's mother, Rosalie Walstrum Lee, who died in 2007, was a behind-the-scenes presence. "My dad was the spotlight," she said. "But he couldn't have done it without my mother." After Tipton's father died when she was fourteen, her mother tried to keep the Penn Hotel going, but, without Bernie Lee's front-of-the house, welcoming demeanor, not as many customers came to dine. "It was depressing," Tipton said. "It was sad."

As might be expected of a building that was constructed in the 1870s, the Penn Hotel had several iterations and building additions over the years. First, the building was the private home of Major John I. Yellott, a lawyer and newspaper editor who served in the Union Army during the Civil

Above: Bernie Lee's Penn Hotel. *Photographer David Turner, courtesy of the Baltimore County Public Library.*

Left: Bernie Lee's Penn Hotel matchbook cover. *Courtesy of Suzanne Loudermilk.*

War. Historians described the house as a brick structure "designed in the fashionable mansard style." Eventually, the building lived up to its name as a hotel after it was sold in the 1920s and used for lodging through the 1930s before becoming a stand-alone restaurant. Its food eventually drew the attention of local critics.

In a 1972 review, the *Baltimore Sun* praised the prime rib as juicy and flavorful, though it declared the rest of the meal uneven, with the oysters described as having "little flavor," and the Caesar salad was panned for having "limp and soggy" lettuce. But when the reviewer John Dorsey returned in 1974 after a change of restaurant management, he found the food improved, writing that the Penn Hotel was an "agreeable place to have dinner." He elaborated on his meal, saying: "[The] shrimp cocktail ($2.95), which, though expensive, was surely one of the finest specimens I've seen anywhere" and that the filet mignon "was slightly overcooked but tender and otherwise satisfactory."

The restaurant sputtered on for a few more years. In 1978, investors, including former Baltimore Colts football players Bobby Boyd and Johnny Unitas, took over, renaming it Baby Doe Mining Co. and adopting a western theme with mining paraphernalia on the walls. *Sun* reviewer, Elizabeth Large, said she felt like she "had stepped into Disney World's 'Frontierland'" on a visit, and, though she didn't like the setting, she found the menu, which included items like prime rib, South African lobster tails and crabmeat quiche, "better than usual." The new restaurant, despite its gimmicky decor and ambitions, closed in 1981 due to financial difficulties and was sold at auction.

The next owner of the property reopened another restaurant and brought back the Penn Hotel name. Its American menu listed Maryland crab soup, rack of lamb, crab imperial, crab cakes and other dishes. Like its immediate predecessors, this restaurant didn't last long either. By 1983, the Penn Hotel was gone, and Armand's Chicago Pizzeria, a family-owned chain restaurant, was slinging deep-dish pies in the Formstone structure.

In the name of progress, the landmark building was finally destroyed by a wrecker's ball in 1989 to make way for Towson Commons, an office-retail-entertainment complex. Now, that building, too, is being updated. But the Penn still remains in the hearts of many. Robert M. Parker Jr., the world-famous wine critic who lives in Parkton, had his first libation there. It wasn't wine but a Roy Rogers child's cocktail. "This is a walk down memory lane," he said while recalling his visits to the Penn Hotel.

23

The Golden Arm

WHERE THE COLTS CAME TO DINE
1968–1995

I n general, Tuesday nights are not bustling with business for restaurants. However, at the Golden Arm, a north Baltimore hot spot that opened in the York Road Plaza shopping center in April 1968, Tuesday nights were prime time for business. "Tuesday was my best night," said Jim Considine, who worked at the Golden Arm in multiple positions, from busboy to bartender and manager. "That was the night Unitas came in." Johnny Unitas, who was then in the glory days of his football career with the Baltimore Colts, co-owned the Golden Arm with fellow Colt Bobby Boyd. Unitas, aka "Johnny U." or the "Golden Arm," was less of a hands-on owner than Boyd, who was in the restaurant nearly every day, but Unitas's reputation as a star football player was a major draw for customers and a thrill for employees. Plus, with photos of Johnny U. in uniform, from his high school days all the way up through his time with the Colts, even when the man wasn't physically in the restaurant, his presence was felt.

Though the legend of Johnny Unitas is a dominating one in Baltimore sports history, those who worked with him at the restaurant don't recall a larger-than-life, outspoken personality. On the contrary: he's remembered as a kind, down-to-earth presence. "I never saw John inebriated or even tipsy. He would have one or two beers," said Jim Considine. "He drank Arrow beer made by the American Brewing Company. When Arrow went out of business, John was devastated." In her memoir *A Peachy Life*, Lenora "Peachy" Dixon, a waitress who worked at the Golden Arm for the first four and a half years it was open, described Unitas as a charismatic guy who wasn't afraid to get his hands dirty. During the restaurant's first weekend in business, there was a problem with the toilets in the ladies' room, but no plumber was called; Johnny U. headed into the restroom, plunger in hand, and dealt with the problem himself. "The women were flabbergasted," Dixon wrote. "They did not know what to do except laugh. Where else could you go and have the famous Johnny Unitas fix your toilet?"

Boyd was a daily presence at the Golden Arm. Though not an overbearing manager, said Considine, he was a smart one. One of Boyd's moves as an owner was to decree that any Baltimore Colt

Johnny Unitas in 1967. *Courtesy of Malcom W. Emmons.*

who ate at the Golden Arm was charged half price, making the restaurant a popular place for the team, especially after home games. With a steady stream of football players coming in, the fans followed—but not always fans of the Colts. Peachy Dixon remembered one away game against the New York Jets when the restaurant was flooded with Jets fans. "All these people came in and sat at the bar and harassed us all day long," she said. "And the worst thing was that they lost the game, and it was awful."

Unitas and his teammates weren't the only local celebrities to turn up at the Golden Arm. Considine recalled spotting a variety of sports stars, including the legendary Oriole, Frank Robinson, and local news personalities, from Marty Bass to Oprah Winfrey, whom he described as a regular and a "gadfly" who could be tough on waitresses.

Many of the noncelebrities who spent time at the Golden Arm were memorable characters in their own right. Rocky Thorton, a lovable bartender with a "wicked sense of humor" was described as having a wildly foul mouth, and Jim Considine said he taught him every swear word he knows. Mr. Foley was a friendly older man, and Peachy Dixon recalled him as something of a surrogate father to Unitas.

Some stretches of time were rowdier than others at the restaurant. Considine remembered one bartender who moonlighted as a bookie, drawing a rough crowd some nights (his actions were not sanctioned by management). But the restaurant was always family-friendly, with parents

Above: Glass from the Golden Arm. *Courtesy of Brennen Jensen.*

Right: Mary T. Michel and Frank Robinson at the Golden Arm. *Courtesy of Jim Considine.*

coming in with kids and older ladies stopping in for Manhattans after their trips to the beauty salon across the street. "It was *Cheers*," said Jim Considine. "It was the local restaurant of Rodgers Forge, Cedarcroft and anybody from the west."

Holidays were big at the Golden Arm. Families visited for Mother's Day, and a more adult crowd congregated for occasions like New Year's Eve and St. Patrick's Day. On those nights, the restaurant drew long lines of people for its $3.17 corned beef and cabbage special.

For all the restaurant's popularity, food was never the big draw. "It never got great reviews," admitted Considine, though he had some favorites on the menu, including the shrimp salad, which he called "the best in Baltimore." The salad came with cooked-to-order shrimp, a dash of Old Bay seasoning and two secret ingredients: Mrs. Filbert's mayonnaise and jarred chicken base. In a 2008 article, *Baltimore Sun* reporter Frederick Rasmussen confirmed that the kitchen would be unlikely to win any Michelin stars. "This was not a place where one would come expecting haute cuisine," he wrote. "Rather, it was the good old-fashioned, stick-to-your-ribs steak and seafood dinners of the 1940s and 1950s that defined dining at the Golden Arm." Other popular dishes included the restaurant's prime rib, oysters casino and shrimp topped with crab imperial—though even those dishes took a backseat to the personalities found in the dining room and at the bar.

The Golden Arm flourished during a time when local sports celebrities typically had jobs in addition to their sports careers—Boyd was a teacher at City College High School along with being a defensive back for the Colts—and many of the bigger names capitalized on their celebrity by going into the restaurant business. Other sports-related restaurants at the time included Art Donovan's Valley Country Club and Gino Marchetti and Alan Amechi's burger chain, Gino's. Both businesses eventually closed but have since been rebooted, under different ownership, in recent years.

In 1988, four years after the Colts left Baltimore, Unitas sold his stake in the restaurant to Bill Grauel, who kept the place alive until St. Patrick's Day in 1995, when its shopping center home was revamped to accommodate a larger grocery store and new tenants.

Unitas died on September 11, 2002. By then, Bobby Boyd had moved back to his native Texas, where he passed away in September 2017. All the old employees and regulars from the Golden Arm days have long since moved on, but the memories of the times they spent together on York Road remain.

24

The Crease

AN ORIGINAL FERN BAR
1972–2016

The Crease in Towson had many lives in its forty-four-year history, from being a trendy fern bar and pub to a raucous college hangout. Its original owner, Richard E. Evans, can be credited with creating a big part of its cherished past. Evans, an All-American University of Virginia lacrosse player turned entrepreneur, opened the Baltimore County spot in 1972 as a place where singles would feel comfortable. The Crease had a dress code (shirts with collars and no jeans), a congenial atmosphere and a casual menu that included specialties like a frenchburger or Crease burger ($2.75) covered in brown gravy, mushrooms and blue cheese; spinach salad (a novelty at the time); sandwiches; and bowls of soups and chili. "The food was simple but tasty," recalled Evans, who is now a Baltimore real estate agent. "Food was the thing to keep you in business." Peggy Fox, Evans's marketing director at the Crease, still keeps in touch with her former boss and remembers his dedication to the menu. "He was such a stickler for the consistency with the food," she said.

A preppy crowd swarmed to the Crease—named after a lacrosse term that refers to the area around each team's goal—and brought with them a thriving nightlife to the once quiet Baltimore County town. On Sundays, when a DJ spun oldies from 9 p.m. to 2 a.m., a line of customers snaked to the 523 York Road entrance, which had no sign for several years. "We would come back from the ocean to go there," said Sunny Gunther, a regular patron who met her late husband, Bill, who was a bartender, there. "It was a different time. You could shoot a cannon at 10 p.m. on York Road [and not hit anyone]."

Baltimore Colts Night guest bartenders at the Crease. *Peggy Fox.*

The restaurant's demographic at the time was also different from what it would be today. From 1974 to 1982, the legal drinking age in Maryland was eighteen, which added teenagers to the mix of customers who would gather at the twenty-seat oak bar, "three and four deep," as Gunther recalled. The bartenders poured drinks like tequila sunrises, Kahlua and creams and jellybean shooters made with peppermint schnapps. "You quickly got to know everyone," said Karen Kiesewetter, who was a frequent customer in the 1970s and early 1980s. "It was like *Cheers* before *Cheers* [existed]." But unlike the banter on the popular sitcom, a rousing rendition of George Thorogood's "Bad to the Bone" at the Crease could lead to dancing on the bar, Kiesewetter said. Patrick Leland, a longtime friend of Evans's, agreed with the *Cheers* analogy and camaraderie. "There were a lot of 'Norms,' or regulars, there," he said, referring to the TV character who spent long hours at the *Cheers* bar. "Everybody knew each other."

Evans also staged many benefit promotions at the bar over the years that attracted local TV personalities like Oprah Winfrey; Orioles players, such as Eddie Murray; and Colts players, including Bert Jones and Bruce Laird. "We liked to do fun events," said Evans.

The Crease also attracted diners with its daily food specials, including half-price burgers and steak and lobster nights. In the early days of the restaurant, the dining area was small, with six tables seating sixteen customers on a raised platform. *Baltimore Sun* restaurant critic Elizabeth Large wrote in a 1976 review: "Neighborhood bars are dim and a little worn around the edges. The Crease is a prettied-up version, so respectable that matrons prefer to have a chicken-salad sandwich at the Crease rather than lunch at Hutzler's tearoom [in the department store across the street]." Large described the tables as having a "high acrylic finish" and mentioned the Tiffany-style lampshades over the bar, adding: "The Crease radiates good taste."

Evans also opened a downtown Crease location in Hopkins Plaza in 1977, but it was later sold in 1982. In 1991, Evans parted with the Towson Crease for personal reasons, but new owners soon took over the restaurant. The purchasers were David and Nathaniel Rugolo, whose late parents, Pietro "Pete" and Beatrice Rugolo, operated Jerry's Belvedere Tavern for many years. At the time, the brothers vowed to keep the Crease the same, although they added dishes like lamb, veal and prime rib to the menu, according to a 1992 *Baltimore Sun* article. Seven years later, another *Baltimore Sun* reviewer wrote that the "traditional bar fare served at the Crease—burgers, wings, sandwiches and steaks—[was] at the top of its class."

As time went by, however, the Crease became increasingly known as a local hangout for college students, and Yelp reviewers began commenting more on the drinks than the food. "Not bad if you are looking to get your cheap drink on," said one review.

The Crease came to its end in 2016, when the business was sold to Erica Russo, the owner of the Point in Fells, a sophisticated pub with New American fare. The renovated space now operates as the Point in Towson.

25

Brass Elephant

AN ELEGANT, HISTORIC SETTING
1977–2009

N ever was there a handsomer restaurant in Baltimore than the Brass Elephant," wrote John Dorsey in a 1980 *Baltimore Sun* review. He wasn't the only diner who admired the stately 1861 townhouse-turned-restaurant. The intricate woodwork, brass-elephant sconces (hence the restaurant's name), crystal chandeliers, marble mantles and exquisite table settings drew *oohs* and *ahs* from scores of visitors during its thirty years of operation in Mount Vernon. *Sun* critic Elizabeth Large also fell under the restaurant's spell: "It was impossible to find much wrong with our surroundings," she wrote in 1980. She described the dining-room as having blue and white linens, glistening goblets, a bouquet of pink carnations and soothing Vivaldi music.

The elegant mansion, originally built as a home for a shipping merchant, had a rich history of homeowners—and the fame of having three toilets, a rarity of the time—until it became an elite furniture store called Potthast Brothers. The store sold expensive, handcrafted mahogany dining tables, chairs and more from the 1930s to the 1970s. The building's fate changed in 1977, when William Paley Jr., the son of the TV executive who built CBS, opened the Brass Elephant restaurant with partners. It got the attention of the syndicated gossip columnist, Suzy, in the *New York Daily News*. She wrote that Baltimore's "social pace quickened—and not a moment too soon," according to the *Washington Post*.

This success did not last for long. The restaurant floundered quickly, ending up at public auction when chef Randy Stahl, who opened Fiori Restaurant in

Left: A dining table at the Brass Elephant. *Courtesy of The Elephant.*

Right: Hallway of the original house. *Courtesy of The Elephant.*

Reisterstown and is a chef instructor at Anne Arundel Community College, bought the building with partners in 1980. He reopened the restaurant the same year, under the same name, offering a mostly northern Italian menu. "Baltimore, at the time, had very few fine-dining options, and it seemed like a natural fit for an elegant, regional Italian restaurant," said Stahl. "Little Italy existed, but the property on Charles Street was ripe for fine Italian dining." The menu of this restaurant included fare like fresh flounder with brown butter, veal cutlet Valdostano, clams posillipo, shrimp marinara, chicken Marengo, saltimbocca, beefsteak Fiorentina and spaghetti carbonara. All of the pastas were handmade. "I can see why it was my mother's favorite 'special occasion' restaurant, or anyone else's for that matter," wrote Shelley Howell, a Towson resident, in her book, *Dining Down Memory Lane*.

The Brass Elephant had its share of big-name guests, including actors Anthony Quinn and Kathleen Turner and singer Paul Simon, who would visit the restaurant while in town for performances at the Morris A. Mechanic Theatre and the Lyric. Winemaker Robert Mondavi celebrated his eightieth birthday at the restaurant with a dozen revelers, Stahl remembered. But Stahl said his most enduring memory is when Pope John Paul II came to

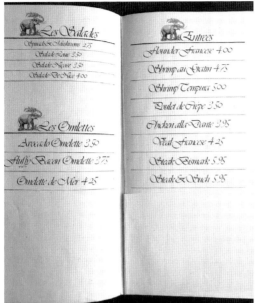

Menu from the Brass Elephant. *Courtesy of The Elephant.*

Baltimore in 1995. The Brass Elephant catered an event at the Baltimore Basilica that included a private luncheon for the papal leader. "He actually met my staff in the courtyard and blessed us," Stahl said.

George Batlas, executive chef at the Manor Tavern in Monkton, worked in the kitchen at the Brass Elephant in the 1980s after graduating from culinary school. He described the restaurant as "very classic," with servers in tuxedoes. For diners, he said, "It was almost like going to the theater." Employees were expected to maintain the decorum. "Everything had to be done a certain way every day," he said. "The uniforms had to be perfect, or you were sent home."

The poor economy in 2007 and the following years hurt the business, Stahl said, and he eventually closed the Brass Elephant in 2009. The last chef was Marcus Olson, who took a more modern approach from the Italian dishes that had been served. He received good reviews from critics, but it wasn't enough to save the restaurant. Olson, who now owns restaurants near Seattle, fondly recalled his time at the Brass Elephant. "I liked the building. I liked the community," he said. "There was a great lineage of people coming there for decades…When it closed, it crushed me."

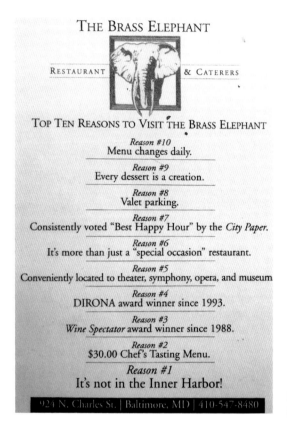

THE BRASS ELEPHANT

RESTAURANT & CATERERS

TOP TEN REASONS TO VISIT THE BRASS ELEPHANT

Reason #10
Menu changes daily.

Reason #9
Every dessert is a creation.

Reason #8
Valet parking.

Reason #7
Consistently voted "Best Happy Hour" by the *City Paper*.

Reason #6
It's more than just a "special occasion" restaurant.

Reason #5
Conveniently located to theater, symphony, opera, and museum

Reason #4
DIRONA award winner since 1993.

Reason #3
Wine Spectator award winner since 1988.

Reason #2
$30.00 Chef's Tasting Menu.

Reason #1
It's not in the Inner Harbor!

924 N. Charles St. | Baltimore, MD | 410-547-8480

Brass Elephant brochure. *Courtesy of The Elephant.*

A nightspot took over the space for a short while before the building was shuttered again, on its way to becoming a forgotten relic. But, in 2015, Steve Rivelis and his wife, Linda Brown Rivelis, took an interest in the property, where they had their wedding thirty years earlier. They had always wanted to open a restaurant. The couple spruced up the rooms, keeping the architectural integrity, before opening a new restaurant called The Elephant in 2016. They wanted a connection to the earlier name, but they also wanted their own identity. "I appreciate the history of the place," Steve Rivelis said. "We want people to treasure, value and appreciate the past. We can build on that and use it as a springboard forward."

Despite their efforts, The Elephant closed in June 2019 due to "legal and financial circumstances," according to a post on the restaurant's website. The stately building is now for sale, waiting for its next chapter.

26

Hersh's Orchard Inn

SPECIAL OCCASION DINING IN THE 'BURBS
1979–1997

Hersh Pachino brought a polished style to the former tavern that sat on the site of a long-ago apple orchard in Towson when he opened Hersh's Orchard Inn in 1979. His personality and charm drew celebrities like entertainer Sammy Davis Jr., actor Tom Selleck, radio and TV personality Larry King and former Orioles pitcher Jim Palmer. "The restaurant was successful because of the guy who owned it," Palmer told the *Baltimore Sun* in 1997. "He understood people and the restaurant business."

The *Sun*'s respected critic John Dorsey also acknowledged Pachino's impact early on: "There is a new owner these past three months or so, and as far as I can tell, he has improved upon a good thing." Pachino's success in the suburbs continued. By 1984, he was named restaurateur of the year by the Restaurant Association of Maryland. He was thrilled when Danny Dickman, the respected owner of the now-closed Danny's restaurant—at one time considered the best restaurant in Baltimore—sent him congratulations by mail. He still has the bright orange greeting card.

Over the years, droves of diners went to the classy white building on busy East Joppa Road for good food and service. In a 1997 *Sun* story, Joe Radebaugh Sr. recalled his many visits with his wife, Bobbie. "They did excellent food with reasonable prices," he said. "Hersh was so personable." Pachino, who learned the tricks of the restaurant trade at Pimlico Hotel as a general manager, took a menu he inherited from the previous owners and added sophisticated nuances. The kitchen turned out dishes like shrimp in garlic butter, stone crabs in season, Chateaubriand for two and stuffed

Hersh's Orchard Inn exterior.
Courtesy of Paul Esbrandt.

lobster tail. Local restaurant reviewers praised the Orchard Inn with comments like: "I was thrilled with my oyster stew, laced with crunchy bits of onion," and "the chicken à la Orchard [was] a wonderfully tender, ivory-white boneless chicken breast arranged with artichoke hearts and fresh mushrooms in a delicate white wine sauce that fairly sang with flavor." The *Sun's* John Dorsey weighed in again in 1985 after the restaurant had been open for several years: "The service and the Maryland-American food—crab, lobster, shrimp, steak, *et cetera*—are still up to the high standards of the Orchard's past."

At the Orchard Inn, which was often considered a special occasion restaurant, Thanksgiving was a big day. Nine hundred customers would show up for the holiday meal, and 75 percent of those customers would order a traditional turkey meal, though entrees like prime rib, surf and turf and imperial crab were also available. Larry King stopped by in November 1996 and was so impressed he inscribed one of the restaurant's special menus with "Thanks for a great Thanksgiving." Pachino, who now lives in Towson, has held on to much of the restaurant's memorabilia, from news clips and menus to old photos. He kept a camera at the restaurant and had his photo taken with a large assortment of friends and stars, from Johnny Unitas and Cal Ripken Jr. to Pam Shriver and Martina Navratilova.

Left: Hersh's Orchard Inn dining room. *Courtesy of Paul Esbrandt.*

Below: Hersh's Orchard Inn menu. *Courtesy of Hersh Pachino.*

In 1989, Pachino opened Ralphie's Diner, which was described as an "upscale Timonium restaurant with 1950s decor" by the *Sun*. The diner was named after Ralph Salvon, the late Orioles trainer. Pachino wanted "a place for employees to move up" as they earned promotions, he said. He prided himself on offering his staff benefits like life insurance and a profit-sharing plan. "I wanted the employees to be successful," he said. "I felt they would stay with me."

After selling the Orchard Inn to Chef Michael Gettier in 1997, Pachino worked at Ralphie's, greeting customers and mentoring workers, such as Stuart Amoriell, who became the restaurant's manager. "I met Hersh, and

Right: Hersh Pachino and Larry King. *Courtesy of Hersh Pachino.*

Below: Hersh Pachino with Cal Ripken Jr. and his parents. *Courtesy of Hersh Pachino.*

he changed the direction of my life," Amoriell said. "He taught me the industry and took me under his wing." Amoriell now runs a restaurant in Lake Placid, New York, with more locations to come—one of which he will be naming Hershel's Deli after his Towson mentor. "It's a testament to him," he said.

Today, the Orchard Inn building has different owners, who have turned it into a casual restaurant called Mo's Seafood. Pachino is no longer involved in operating restaurants, but he runs a restaurant-consulting business and continues the charity work he has done through the years. "I loved it, but it was tough," said Pachino, a father of three who worked ten- to twelve-hour days at the restaurants. "I had a good run."

27

Gampy's

INTRODUCING AN ECLECTIC MENU
1979–1995

Gampy's in Mount Vernon was a pioneering restaurant when it opened in 1979 with its innovative, cartoon-styled menu that offered Baltimoreans a mix of cuisines. Its name was even an acronym for the "Great American Melting Pot." "We worked on the concept for two years," said Don Friedman, who owned the restaurant with his father, Philip Friedman. "It had an eclectic approach to American cuisine." The kitchen prepared a number of unique dishes, including quiche, chilies con queso, teriyaki vegetables, fondue, fajitas, beef Wellington and a burger with guacamole. The selections, sometimes described as upscale diner food, had crazy names like Bongo Bongo soup (a Polynesian puree of oyster soup), Illegal French toast and Wild West spareribs. But probably nothing was more popular than the restaurant's three-decker Monte Cristo sandwich with ham, cheese, turkey and Melba sauce.

"Gampy's was one of the first restaurants around here to offer foods of different ethnic backgrounds, which was a pretty original concept when the place opened some 15 years ago," a *Baltimore Sun* reviewer wrote in 1993. The restaurant also introduced selling beef by the ounce. "My father thought you should have the best meat for the dollar," Friedman said. "We were proud of our steak."

The father-son team, whose family operated the esteemed Chesapeake Restaurant on North Charles Street from 1933 to 1986, marketed Gampy's with catchy slogans like "Just Eat It," "Try a Fresh Thing" and "Eat Naked." "We were very edgy," said Don Friedman, who now lives in Las Vegas. "It

Above: Gampy's opening menu from 1979. *Courtesy of Don Friedman.*

Right: Gampy's menu from 1988. *Courtesy of Don Friedman.*

was a different style than what people were used to," Friedman said. "The kitchen was like a well-stocked kitchen at your house; steaks, burgers, but, most important, we wanted to create an experience."

Thea Osato worked at Gampy's as a waitress for three years in the 1980s and remembers her boss, Don Friedman, well. "He was the funniest guy ever," she said. "He was fun to work with. He was very dear." Osato still keeps in touch with many of the restaurant's former employees, who bonded over dealing with customers and working long shifts that could last until three o'clock in the morning. After last call at Baltimore bars,

Gampy's dining room. *Courtesy of Don Friedman.*

hungry hordes would often head to Gampy's for late-night snacks. "It was a colorful place to work," said Osato, who never got used to the buttons the staff had to wear on their uniforms, especially one that said, "Our skins are hot." "I met more people that I still know and love. I met so many wonderful people there."

The ambiance of the restaurant was sophisticated but unpretentious. Don Friedman said, "We wanted the restaurant to be a place where people could enjoy each other's company." The atmosphere, along with the 1960s music and the décor—upholstered dark blue–patterned banquettes, emerald-green sconces and reflective Mylar ceiling (later becoming red-and-blue neon zigzags)—drew local residents and celebrities like Ricki Lake, Sally Struthers, Chita Rivera and Julia Louis-Dreyfus. "What makes Gampy's and places like it enduringly popular is that they offer a good selection of interesting dishes for people who want a few more choices than just hamburgers and pizza for under $10," wrote Elizabeth Large in a 1993 *Sun* review. "Gampy's does have hamburgers and pizza, but the pizza, for instance, is an individual one with toppings like Boursin and bacon. The thick, 8-inch crust (a bit too thick for my taste) is slathered with rich, herb-flavored cream cheese."

By the time Gampy's closed in 1995, Don Friedman was beginning to be ground down. "It started to be work," he said. "It became more of a grind." However, he still thinks about those restaurant days with affection, saying, "I have so many memories of coming in and having fun."

28

Harvey's at Green Spring Station

A HOT SPOT IN BALTIMORE COUNTY
1979–2000

Chef and owner Harvey Shugarman birthed his eponymous Harvey's at Green Spring Station with big dreams and a big vision. His restaurant grew from a small space in an upscale retail center in 1979 to an enterprise with dining rooms, a bar, a gourmet shop, banquet rooms and catering services when it closed twenty years later. "It grew exponentially," said Barry Baumel, who worked at Harvey's as a kitchen manager after his family's restaurant Harvey House closed in 1993. "It was one busy place. It was multifaceted." The restaurant's Baltimore County location in Lutherville, just outside the Baltimore Beltway, was popular from the beginning with an eclectic menu, outdoor patio and Shugarman's presence. "He had a great personality," Baumel said. "I was always looking to open a restaurant," said Shugarman, who worked as a general manager at Girard's Disco, a popular dance-and-café spot in Mount Vernon, before overseeing Harvey's. "I had a sense of the area and what it could be."

When Shugarman planned Harvey's, he also devised a food lineup to attract customers—from local residents to office workers at the multiuse complex. "I knew I had to have variety on the menu," he said. "It could be something for everyone." He opened the sixty-seat restaurant with 130 items. "We had amazing talent in the kitchen," he said. "Everything was freshly prepared. We did our own butchery, made our own stocks, at a good price."

As business grew, so did the space; Shugarman added a full-service bar and acquired a full liquor license. Seating in the restaurant also increased

Harvey's at Greenspring. *Photographer Clement D. Erhardt Jr., courtesy of Baltimore County Public Library.*

with two expansions: first to 125 seats and then to 250 seats. "Harvey's is an informal establishment, offering an imaginative blend of classical American and foreign-styled dishes," wrote reviewer Joe D'Adamo for the *Evening Sun* in 1984. "It's possible to build a very exciting and different meal at Harvey's." The *Baltimore Sun*'s critic Carleton Jones described the restaurant's crab cake on an English muffin as "large and luscious with crab" in 1982. He also noted how noisy and "full of families with kids" the restaurant was, but he added: "In its price range and format, it may be unrivaled in the north end." Another of the *Sun*'s reviewers, Elizabeth Large, praised the fare. "The menu seemed so full of good ideas. The food sounded jazzy and fun and promising," she wrote in 1992. "I liked the setting. If you're lucky, the weather will be nice, and you can eat in the courtyard."

The menu included burgers; pastas, like ravioli with ricotta and spinach; sandwiches; pizzas; charbroiled fish; Cajun barbecued chicken; a section called "Dieter's Dreams"; and Asian dishes, including egg rolls, chicken Szechuan and peanut-and-sesame-seed noodles. A chef who worked at the landmark Pimlico Hotel restaurant in Pikesville made the "best Chinese food" at Harvey's, Baumel said. Harvey's also offered Sunday brunch before the weekend midday meal was mainstream. A pastry chef was also in the restaurant's kitchen, turning out desserts like a peanut butter bombe with chocolate sauce and whipped cream, a lemon mousse with raspberry sauce and chocolate paté. Another well-liked item at Harvey's was the Coffey salad, which, as mentioned in chapter fourteen, was named after Claudia Coffey, a longtime Pimlico Hotel waitress who created the salad: a mix of

Above: The courtyard at Harvey's at Green Spring Station. *Courtesy of Harvey Shugarman.*

Opposite, top: The gourmet shop at Harvey's at Green Spring Station. *Courtesy of Harvey Shugarman.*

Opposite, bottom: A dining room at Harvey's at Green Spring Station. *Courtesy of Harvey Shugarman.*

iceberg lettuce, hard-boiled egg, onion, tomato, garlic, oregano, Parmesan cheese, anchovies and oil and vinegar. "It was a huge seller," Shugarman said. "When the Pimlico closed, I asked if I could have permission to make it. [Coffey said she] was cool with that."

After two decades, Shugarman closed Harvey's and focused on restaurant consulting; then, he "started playing with chocolate." Today, he's fashioning artisan chocolates at Shugarman's Little Chocolate Shop in Madrid, New Mexico, a "hippie" town he said he fell madly in love with. "It's real funky. It's real small. I bring my dog to work every day." He still appreciates his days at Harvey's: "I don't have one regret," he said. "It was a great experience."

29

Louie's Bookstore Café

FOOD WITH AN ARTISTIC TWIST
1981–2001

In the early 1980s, long before Amazon was a household name or e-readers were a thing, a much smaller bookstore revolution was taking place in Mount Vernon at Louie's Bookstore Café. From the start, the bookstore and café drew an eclectic crowd that loved it for its artsy vibe and likable food. In a 1984 article, *Baltimore Sun* writer Lynn Williams described Louie's as "an upscale version of one of those Greenwich Village literary cafes." The magic of the café started on the street, when passersby peeked into Louie's, which faced a busy section of Charles Street. They would see the work of artist Thea Osato, who spent years decorating the bookstore and café's windows with creative displays, hinting at the jumble of music, books and food found inside. The café's interior was just as intriguing; it was decked out with Victorian mirrors, red walls, local art and—just inside the entrance—lots and lots of books.

"Having a bookstore upfront was something very special," said Richard Gorelick, a former restaurant critic for the *Baltimore Sun* and *City Paper* and a frequent customer at Louie's. "It was a good bookstore, and you could spend time browsing and go read at the bar. I spent a lot of time at the bar by myself, mostly with just a cup of coffee and a sandwich."

Louie's was the brainchild of Jimmy Rouse, an artist and son of James W. Rouse, the developer famous for the planned community of Columbia and Harborplace downtown. Rouse had been waiting tables at Martick's Restaurant Francais when C. William "Bill" Struever, a Martick's regular, mentioned that the Charles Street bookstore and café, Kramer Books,

This page and opposite: Front window at Louie's Bookstore Café. *Courtesy of Thea Osato.*

was going out of business and needed someone to take it over. "I thought, 'This is a great idea, what Baltimore needs,'" recalled Rouse. "But they had Washington prices and a Washington menu. No crab cake, nothing local and it was priced too high." One thing led to another, and, within a few weeks, Rouse left Martick's (on good terms) and purchased Kramer Books's inventory and took over its loans. He had help—a former chef from Martick's and her boyfriend, a waiter and maître d' from the Brass Elephant. They did some quick redecorating, like removing the glass tops from tables and installing chandeliers purchased from an Eastern shore antique sale, and, in 1981, just two weeks after Rouse's last day at Martick's, he opened Louie's, which he named after his young son.

"[Louie's] was shaped by Jimmy Rouse," recalled William Zvarick, who worked at Louie's as a server and bartender for around twelve years, starting in the mid-1980s. "He had this vision—he was an artistic spirit in his own personality. He wanted to have a restaurant where he hired a bunch of artists, so it made for an interesting staff." Zvarick, who was a musician himself, said Rouse's idea worked. "It was an interesting bunch of people," he said. The staff may have been "interesting," but even they admit that their quirks didn't always make for the best service. Then again, some considered that part of Louie's charm. "Artists are all left-handed and dyslexic—it's a cliché but kind of true. So, [Louie's] was known for having really terrible service," said Zvarick. "You had to wait forever to get food and sometimes waiters were a little abusive—but not me! It had this dubious reputation and people joked that people kept coming in for the abuse."

The opportunity to mingle with local artists and musicians made the questionable service worth it. Louie's walls were an ever-changing gallery of local artwork (often including pieces by the staff), and the bookstore and café was also a venue for frequent, impromptu concerts. "Peabody students would wander in," recalled Zvarick. "A guitarist, a friend who played piano, a flutist, every now and then, a singer. I sat down and played a few times myself."

As much as the books, art and people drove Louie's notoriety, the food wasn't an afterthought. "It was a pretty basic menu. People came in for potato skins or fried mushrooms or falafel. Simple food, but good recipes," said Zvarick. Puff pastry crab tarts, artichoke hearts with hummus and "Chestertown Chicken," a Rouse family recipe for chicken marinated in ginger, curry and lemon, were popular orders. The café's entrées changed daily, and the desserts were freshly baked from scratch. When the restaurant

Front window at Louie's Bookstore Café. *Courtesy of Thea Osato.*

first opened, the crew purchased desserts from an outside vendor, but, quickly, Rouse realized they should make them in-house. "In a few years, I had four full-time bakers and we had twenty-five desserts, plus specials," he said. "That became a huge part of our business." Zvarik most fondly remembers a white chocolate pound cake, which he ate regularly, topped with chocolate ice cream, as his standard shift meal. Aside from Zvarick, that pound cake had a lot of fans. "First and foremost was the dessert display in the back. I remember the ritual of walking back through the dining room and inspecting that evening's desserts," said Gorelick. "The white chocolate pound cake was a revelation for me—just how dense and luscious and moist that cake was."

In the days before lattes were available on every corner, Louie's coffee was also a draw. "We had a very busy cappuccino bar," said Zvarick. "Long before Starbucks came along, we would sling hundreds of cappuccinos and mochas out of that espresso machine. It was one of the first places I [knew] in Baltimore where that whole 'caffeine' thing was happening."

This page: Front window at Louie's Bookstore Café. *Courtesy of Thea Osato.*

Along with being known as a great place to spend time alone, Louie's was known as a late-night destination for groups of friends. "You could go only for dessert and coffee and make an evening of it, feel like you were part of a scene, downtown in the theater and arts district. People would be going over there from Center Stage or the symphony or art galleries," Gorelick said. In a 1984 *Baltimore Sun* article about late night food, writer Lynn Williams wrote that Louie's was "one of those rare places that often [attracted] more customers late at night than at a more conventional dinner hour." The customers in question weren't just Baltimore's artsy set, either. "Everyone in Baltimore went there at some point. Every restaurant has regulars. We had a regular crowd, but it was really everybody," said Zvarick.

"Every month was better than the previous month for twelve years in a row, when we started to plateau a bit. It was always a profitable business. I was lucky that way," said Rouse. As popular as the restaurant was during the 1980s and 1990s, its star didn't shine forever; when it started to fade, it did so gradually. In 1998, Rouse was ready to get out of the restaurant business and transition to working on his art full time. That year, he sold Louie's to John DeLauro and Catherine Ronalds-DeLauro, but he retained ownership of the building, financed the deal and stayed involved in the operation to some degree; he still chose art for the walls. Ronalds-DeLauro's father, Hugh Ronalds, was, at the time, a Bolton Hill resident and a Louie's customer. His daughter was the catering manager at the Hôtel Plaza Athénée in New York. The couple moved into a downtown Baltimore apartment when they took over ownership of the café.

A restaurant review published shortly after the change in ownership reported that not much changed following that sale: the menu included a few new dishes, but the space and atmosphere remained the same. However, the café didn't remain open long under Ronalds-DeLauro management. In September 1999, the *Sun* reported that Louie's had closed but that Rouse was working on a deal with Biagio Scotto, the owner of an Italian restaurant in York, Pennsylvania. The Ronalds-DeLauros blamed the business's failure, at least in part, on the changing nature of the bookstore business. At the time, large national bookstore chains like Barnes and Noble were booming and grabbing market share from smaller, independent shops.

When Scotto took over the restaurant in 1999, he updated the menu and removed the books altogether. The result was unpopular with the café's regulars, and his tenure as owner was short-lived. "It had a slow death," said Gorelick. "Sometimes those lingering restaurant deaths are the worst because you don't get to say a proper goodbye." In 2001, Papermoon Diner owner Un Kim bought the Louie's building from Jimmy Rouse and his partners. Kim abandoned the Louie's brand, and opened Ixia instead, a glam supper club that occupied the space until 2009.

In the years since then, the space has housed a restaurant and a club, but nothing has been as memorable or unique as Louie's. The bookstore and café's influence on Baltimore remains strong today. Most notably, in 2016, restaurateur Spike Gjerde partnered with Ann and Ed Berlin, the owners of the Ivy Bookshop, to open Bird in Hand, a Charles Village bookstore and café inspired by Louie's. "Everyone keeps saying, 'Oh my God, we need a Louie's,'" Ed Berlin told the *Sun*, just prior to Bird in Hand's opening. But even Bird in the Hand's biggest fans agree that there was something magical about Louie's that can't be replicated. "The whole thing worked in a weird way," said Zvarick. "I've worked in a bunch of restaurants, but Louie's had this sort of alchemy. It just worked."

30

Jeannier's

A CLASSIC FRENCH RESTAURANT
1986–2005

By the time Jeannier's opened in 1986, Americans were several decades into their Julia Child–fueled love affair with French cooking and the restaurant's chef and owner, Roland Jeannier. It's not a surprise, then, that, even in Jeannier's early days, the restaurant had a quality to it that made it feel like it had been open for forever.

Roland Jeannier was born in Provence and began cooking around age fifteen. At one point, he was a French army chef before he and his wife, Colette, moved to the United States in the late 1950s. They first landed in Boston before heading south to Baltimore in the early 1960s. His first job in town was at Les Tuilieries in the Stafford Hotel in Mount Vernon. During his early years in the Baltimore area, Jeannier worked in a number of different restaurants before eventually becoming a chef and part-owner at Country Fare Inn. At that time, he also advised several other restaurants owned by his business partners, including Fiori, King's Contrivance and the Brass Elephant. In the early 1980s, he sold his share of Country Fare Inn and decamped for St. Paul, Minnesota, for two years. A noncompete agreement with his former Country Fare partners meant he couldn't work in the Baltimore-Washington region during that time. In 1985, he returned to Baltimore and bought the restaurant that would become Jeannier's.

Located in the Broadview, a midcentury apartment building in the quiet, upscale Tuscany-Canterbury neighborhood near Johns Hopkins University's Homewood campus, Jeannier's served classic country French fare out of a comfortable, and conservative, dining room. Before Roland

Jeannier took the building over, the Broadview restaurant space was a staid apartment building dining room, the kind of place that hosted "long, slow Sunday dinners with crab imperial and iced tea and Jell-O salad," wrote restaurant critic Elizabeth Large in a 1994 *Baltimore Sun* article. But when Jeannier took over the space, he enlisted his wife to handle the interior design. She overhauled the restaurant, "transforming the formerly dark closed-in space into a series of bright, airy rooms completely redecorated in shades of soft mauve and beige," according to a 1986 article by *Sun* reporter Linda Lowe Morris.

Right away, Jeannier's made a splash in the Baltimore restaurant scene. A couple months after Jeannier's opened, the *Sun* reviewed it. The critic, Carleton Jones, loved the food, and gave high praise to the terrine de canard, a "highly original" crab and sorrel dish, and the quenelle de brochet a la Lyonnaise, "large but light little poached pikefish puddings, superbly jacketed in French pastry in the form of a fish and napped in a buttery, lobster sauce." The *Sun*'s restaurant critic, John Dorsey, mentioned Jeannier's in a December 1986 article listing the best restaurants that opened that year. "It's earning the success it deserves," he wrote. "What Mr. Jeannier does, he does well: duck terrine, snails, quenelles, ragout of seafood with sorrel sauce, etc. This would be a winner any year."

The restaurant's space, though recently spruced up, wasn't as unequivocal a hit. Jones called the room "preposterously frumpy," and, after a 1988 visit, *Sun* writer Lynn Williams described the restaurant as "stodgy and bourgeois." Elizabeth Large was more diplomatic in her 1994 article, where she described the space as having "comfortable, conservative rooms" that were "rather formal," but she also noted that the clientele tended to be on the conservative side. During that visit, Large was enthusiastic about Jeannier's sauces: "The hollandaise was so delicate and lemon-buttery that even a tree branch would have tasted good." She also described the restaurant's signature dessert: the oeufs a la neige, with its "cloud of poached meringue surrounded by a halo of caramelized spun sugar" floating in a "delicate, vanilla-scented crème anglaise."

Despite the flowery descriptions of Roland Jeannier's food, the restaurant was also perceived as fairly approachable. "It was one of the first accessible French restaurants," said longtime Baltimorean Meg Fairfax Fielding, noting that it wasn't the only French restaurant in the city but that it felt like an "easier" option for people than Martick's downtown location. The location was part of that comfort, Fielding recalled, but it was also Roland Jeannier, his staff and the environment they created. "It had a very familial

Former home of Jeannier's. *Courtesy of Kit Pollard.*

atmosphere," she said. "[The restaurant was] more country French than city French. It was very convivial. There was a group of people who were just there all the time, which, I think, is a mark of a really good restaurant."

For years, there were two types of Baltimore diners (maybe there still are). In one camp, you had the people who loved everything exactly as it always was and never wanted anything to change. In the other, you had Baltimoreans who actively sought out whatever was new and next. Jeannier's was always more of a go-to option for the more conservative, leave-my-favorite-restaurant-alone set, but in its prime, the restaurant seemed to satisfy both types of food enthusiasts. Though it never made sweeping changes to the main menu, in the mid-1990s, Jeannier's added a more casual—and less expensive—bar menu that featured dishes like salads, omelets, French bread pizza and a soft-shell crab sandwich.

By the dawn of the twenty-first century, the neighborhood around the restaurant was starting to evolve in terms of restaurant offerings. In her February 2000 review of Jeannier's, Elizabeth Large noted that new and exciting spots were popping up in the Homewood-Roland Park corridor, including the One World Café and the transformation of the Ambassador into an Indian restaurant. "In the middle of all this excitement is an oasis of *terrine de canard* and *oeufs à la neige* known as Jeannier's," she wrote. Large wasn't complaining, but she did observe that Jeannier's was something of a time capsule, transporting diners to the era of Julia Child. Still, she said she enjoyed her meal immensely, writing: "Jeannier's is the place to go when you feel like indulging in rich sauces, scalloped potatoes and sweet butter, with hardly a green vegetable in sight."

When Jeannier's closed in 2005, it was replaced by another French restaurant, Brasserie Tatin, which was owned by maître d' Marc Dettori and Gerard Billebault, who, along with his wife, Gayle Brier, now owns Bonjour Bakery on Falls Road. Billebault approached Roland Jeannier about selling the restaurant to him, though, according to his telling, convincing Jeannier to sell wasn't too challenging. "I had to talk Roland into it, but I did not have to talk too much," Billebault told the *Sun*. Jeannier's sons were not interested in the restaurant business and his wife, Colette, a custom dressmaker who handled the original redecoration and continued to arrange flowers, grow herbs and help as hostess for the restaurant, had passed away in 1994.

Brasserie Tatin wasn't a carbon copy of Jeannier; it had a more modern and casual sensibility, with grilled items and late-night desserts. It also didn't have the staying power. Tatin closed in 2008 and was replaced by the Italian restaurant, La Famiglia, which was open from 2008 to 2015. Today, the space is occupied by Cypriana, a Greek restaurant that opened in 2017 and does a bustling business.

In a 2007 "whatever happened to" column, the *Sun's* Frederick Rasmussen caught up with Jeannier. He said he was enjoying retirement—he had just taken a trip to France to visit some of his grandchildren and was, at the time, planning a Thanksgiving dinner celebration—but he also admitted he missed the restaurant and its regular customers. Jeannier later remarried and has slipped out of the public eye, but he is certainly not forgotten.

31

Polo Grill

A CLUBBY CLASSIC
1990–2002

From the day it opened in 1990, the Polo Grill was the place to be. Reservations were hard to come by at the Hopkins-area hot spot, and right away, it drew boldfaced names and beautiful people. The restaurant was a part of the Inn at the Colonnade, an imposing University Parkway hotel and condo building that was constructed in the late 1980s. With a masculine, clubby vibe and creative menu, it earned its popularity easily.

The restaurant was the brainchild of Lenny and Gail Kaplan, a Baltimore restaurant power couple with deep roots. Gail's father was Leon Shavitz, the legendary owner of the Pimlico Hotel; she grew up in that restaurant. Lenny had been involved in running Pimlico Hotel since he and Gail were married in 1959. "Gail and Lenny, who everybody knew and they knew everybody. That was their big foray into fine dining," said lifelong Baltimorean Meg Fairfax Fielding. The Polo Grill concept was inspired by Lenny Kaplan's late 1980s visit to San Francisco's Stars restaurant. Stars was known for being simultaneously opulent and comfortable and for courting an A-list crowd; the Kaplans, drawing on their experience and connections, set about creating a Baltimore version of the same.

Polo Grill's executive chef Harold Marmulstein was heralded as a genius for his menu full of dishes that had classic roots but incorporated trendy touches. Critics praised the famous fried lobster tail, blackened pork chop in raspberry sauce and grilled chicken with roasted garlic, tomatoes and balsamic vinegar. Desserts, also, were a specialty of the house. The fried

Inn at the Colonnade, former home of the Polo Grill. *Courtesy of Kit Pollard.*

lobster tail was "all succulent sweetness, without a touch of grease," raved Lynn Williams in the *Baltimore Sun's* 1990 dining guide. "Desserts are to die for, whether you choose an angelically sweet Paris-Brest or a chocolate-pistachio terrine black and bitter and sexy as sin," she wrote. The restaurant's dishes may have occasionally been a little too elaborate, critics admitted, but overall, the food was approachable and satisfying.

The Rita St. Clair–designed space made an even more lasting impression than the menu. Reporters writing about the place frequently referenced Ralph Lauren—a huge fashion and lifestyle brand at the time—and praised its "clubby" vibe, while also noting that it was not as pretentious as the look might suggest. "It was so swank and fancy," said Fielding. "It was all very hunt country, very equestrian." Reviewing for the *Sun* just after the restaurant's opening, Janice Baker complimented the walls, which were "covered in deep paisley and dark green, and black table lamps topped with brass animal heads." Also in the *Sun,* Lynn Williams observed that "those smart entrepreneurs who developed...the Polo Grill, knew that if they garnished their rooms with haute-WASP [white, Anglo-Saxon, protestant] trappings—polished cherry wood, paisley, paintings of horses and dogs—

aristocracy-hungry Baltimoreans would flock." And flock they did—not only for the food and atmosphere but also for the owners.

Gail Kaplan's father, Leon Shavitz, was famous for his impact on Baltimore's midcentury dining scene. Following in his father-in-law's footsteps, Lenny became a legend in his own right, known for his exacting standards and often demanding approach to management. Gail Kaplan was the yin to Lenny's yang. "If Mr. Kaplan's all business, she's pure pleasure," wrote Mary Corey in a 1990 profile of the pair. "She purrs along, a petite dynamo in Giorgio Armani glasses, a navy suit and heels." Corey called Gail "more vivacious than a high school cheerleader," but she was also quick to praise her organizational skills. Gail, for her part, recognized that, as a woman at that time, she was at something of a disadvantage in the business. "Sometimes I get angry that I'm still the wife, although I work just as hard as he does," Kaplan told Corey.

Lenny Kaplan was a tough boss, but he also had a core understanding of the importance of excellent service and maintaining a keen focus on relationships with guests. "The hazard is that the owner forgets…where his roots are, and he doesn't take care of his old regulars," Kaplan told Corey. "All of a sudden, he's caught up in this romantic, glamorous in-spot concept…that is the kiss of death. If you make commitments to the people that support you on a regular basis, you won't be a flash in the pan." He started developing those types of relationships at the Pimlico Hotel, and they paid off when he and Gail opened a place of their own. Baltimore native Merle Porter and her family were some of the guests who followed the Kaplans from the Pimlico Hotel to their new venture. "We went a lot because we already knew Lenny from the Pimlico," she remembered. "We ate there a lot. It was just really nice and the kind of place where, since we knew Lenny, we could usually get a table."

Lenny Kaplan tested those relationships in 1993, when he instituted a no-smoking policy in the restaurant. He admitted, at the time, that it might be costing him some customers, but he held firm. The rest of the restaurant industry was slow to catch up, but, eventually, smoking was banned in restaurants and bars across Maryland in 2008. Even with the ban on smoking, people kept coming. For much of its time in the limelight, the biggest complaint registered about the Polo Grill was that it was *too* crowded, which meant that it could be noisy. "You will have to pass through an often-crowded bar to get to the dining room, and on weekends, the noise level can be discouraging," wrote Lynn Williams in the *Sun* in 1990. "If you can deal with those aggravations, you'll be in for dinner that is to the manor born."

During the Polo Grill years, the Kaplans didn't stand still for very long; they didn't have time. During that era, they were also operating Classic Catering (Gail Kaplan is still involved with that company today), and in 1998, they opened Lenny's Chop House in Harbor Inn Pier 5, though it closed just a year later. The official story was that the restaurant closed when Kaplan couldn't reach a business agreement with the new owner of the hotel, John Paterakis Sr., though several years after its closing, Kaplan ended up paying a settlement following a lawsuit for nonpayment of rent.

The lifespan of Baltimore restaurants seemed to speed up during the latter part of the twentieth century. In a quick ten years, the Polo Grill went from being a trendy new hot spot where reservations were hard to come by to being "one of the last of Baltimore's Grand Old Restaurants," as Elizabeth Large called it in the *Sun* in 1991. In his article written on the eve of the restaurant's closing, the *Sun's* Arthur Hirsch observed the Polo Grill's trajectory: "The Polo Grill thrived through its first year," he wrote. "Trouble began as the restaurant approached its tenth year, an anniversary that 99 percent of restaurants do not live to celebrate."

Executive chef Harold Marmulstein helmed the kitchen from the restaurant's opening in 1990 until 1995, when Jonathan Charmatz, a Polo Grill veteran, took over and Marmulstein moved to Atlanta to open a new restaurant. A year later, another chef, Thomas Brown, took over. At that point, kitchen turnover got even speedier. From 1999 through the restaurant's final night, New Year's Eve 2002, the restaurant employed seven different executive chefs.

Just like Lenny's father-in-law, Leon Shavitz, passed the reins of the Pimlico Hotel to him, when it was time to close the doors of the Polo Grill, the keys were turned over to the Kaplan's son-in-law, Rob Freeman. Freeman transformed the space into a new concept, Four West, but it didn't last for long. Freeman was out of the restaurant business by the end of 2004. The restaurant was, for a short stint, run by the food service company Aramark, which was also managing the hotel property, and in 2006, a team of restaurateurs and marketing folks opened the Spice Company in the space. Two and a half years later, that, too, closed. Since March 2009, the bistro Alizée has been open and operating in the space.

Though Gail is still involved in Classic Catering, the Kaplans have largely stepped away from the restaurant spotlight. But they're certainly not forgotten by their old fans. In less than thirteen years, they put their clubby, Ralph Lauren–style stamp on the city.

32

Spike & Charlie's

ELEVATING THE CULINARY SCENE
1991–2004

These days, the name "Gjerde" is so closely entwined with Baltimore restaurants that it's hard to remember a time before Spike and Charlie, the brothers Gjerde, had made their mark on the local culinary scene. But, in 1991, when the Gjerdes opened Spike & Charlie's Restaurant and Wine Bar, there was no Woodberry Kitchen (the farm-to-table spot that's made Spike famous) or Papi's, Wicked Sisters, Huck's American Craft or Alexander's Tavern (the casual restaurants, sprinkled across the city, that Charlie co-owns).

The Spike & Charlie's origin story is a family tale in every way. After college, Spike worked at the venerable pastry shop Patisserie Poupon, Café des Artistes, Restaurant 2110 and the Center Club as a pastry chef. Charlie, after a brief stint of doing deliveries for Patisserie Poupon, managed a LensCrafters. Despite their lack of broad restaurant experience, the brothers, who grew up in Cockeysville, wanted to open a place of their own. Their parents were on board and were willing to invest. The plan fell into place when their father, David, who was then a Procter & Gamble executive, met the real estate mogul C. William "Bill" Struever through a wine tasting group at Pinehurst Wine Shoppe.

Finding the right location for the venture was a challenge. "I would've signed any lease you put in front me, I was so ready to go," said Spike Gjerde. The family was in negotiations for a spot in Brown's Arcade downtown, but it wasn't going anywhere. Struever then showed the family a closed, former jazz club near the Meyerhoff Symphony Hall.

"There were still beers in the fridge," said Spike. "We sat at the bar there, and we had a handshake deal in about fifteen minutes; and we were off to the races."

Spike, the intellectual culinary creative, ran the kitchen, while Charlie, the more business-oriented and laid-back of the pair, handled the front-of-house operations. Their father managed the wine program and helped with the business end of things and their mother, Alice, worked with Charlie as a hostess.

When the restaurant opened in 1991, Spike & Charlie's introduced Baltimore to a new kind of dining. Spike said:

> *It felt to me like a pivotal moment in restaurants in Baltimore. A lot of the grand old restaurants were still holding sway—Haussner's, the Chesapeake, Marconi's, Danny's and Tio Pepe's. They represented a connection to the great tradition of Baltimore dining that was starting to fade away. The conventions of dining that they represented that were more formal and tradition-bound were very much still present.*

Enter the Gjerdes. "I had a very different idea that was more in line with Chez Panisse and Al Forno in Providence, Rhode Island. They were my biggest influences," Spike said. This meant that Spike & Charlie's would have more casual food, like pizzas cooked in a wood-burning oven, would focus on ingredients and would have a constantly evolving menu.

Spike headed to the Waverly farmers' market on Saturday mornings and to the market under the JFX on Sundays to fill his backseat with ingredients for the week. During those trips, he began building the relationships with farmers. He still has many of those relationships, and they have helped him propel Woodberry Kitchen to success.

Baltimore ate it up—both the creative food and the fun, cool atmosphere. In a 1991 article written just after the restaurant opened, the *Baltimore Sun's* Mary Corey wrote about the restaurant's "funky décor—local papier maché art, steel mesh candleholders and Villeroy & Boch dinnerware," but called it "all a foil for Mr. (Spike) Gjerde's real passion: New American cuisine." In the 1995 "best restaurants" issue of *Baltimore* magazine, Spike & Charlie's was described as a "hip, brightly lit restaurant/gallery" with an ever-changing menu and food, like spicy pumpkin soup and seared tuna pizza, that is "progressive American." The *Baltimore Sun's* 1997 dining guide praised the homemade bread and "très trendy pizzas." The desserts, which were constantly changing, also had a legion of fans.

Spike & Charlie's dinner menu (*left*) and lunch menu (*right*). *Courtesy of Charlie Gjerde.*

The restaurant's focus on wine was also something new for Baltimoreans. "Most Baltimore wine lists still didn't feature much in the way of vintages, and there were still wine lists that had Chablis and Burgundy that came in from California in giant jugs," said Spike. Spike & Charlie's partnered with local wine aficionados, like David Wells, who is now one of the owners of the Wine Source in Hampden, and the late Nelson Carey, who, at the time, managed North Charles Fine Wines and went on to open Grand Cru in Belvedere Square with Spike. Together, they met winemakers and hosted numerous wine dinners. At one point, the restaurant even had its own wine. "It was a time of tremendous discovery and awakening for food and cuisine," said Spike. "I felt that Spike & Charlie's in its own small way was part of that. To this day, I'm proud of that."

While Spike focused on the kitchen, Charlie was busy navigating the business and front-of-house aspects of the restaurant. Opening a restaurant across the street from a theater offered a built-in base of guests, but it also came with some logistical challenges. "One hundred and fifty people wanted to come in…get sat by 6:15 and be out by 7:45," said Charlie. "The real challenge was trying to pace people coming in and getting the food out. That was the most stressful fourteen years of my life. My job was basically to walk around and calm people down." Juggling the timing with Spike's emphasis on fresh ingredients was especially difficult. "Everything was cooked from scratch, even stuff like mashed potatoes, he would cook in small orders," said Charlie. In addition to the theater crowd, Spike & Charlie's high profile and reputation would draw in local celebrities and those coming to town to perform, from Martin O'Malley to Jerry Seinfeld. One of Charlie Gjerde's most notable memories of the time was when Yo-Yo Ma, a frequent guest at Spike & Charlie's, pulled out his cello to play "Happy Birthday" to another guest. "That was awesome," he said.

Spike & Charlie's was popular, but it wasn't a restaurant for everyone. In the 1992 *Sun* dining guide, Elizabeth Large recounted a tale about recommending the place to an acquaintance, only to have him complain that he couldn't get ranch for his salad. In 1994, she wrote, "Who will love S&C's? Anyone who admires creative cuisine, enjoys theatrical surroundings, thinks smallish portions are a blessing rather than a rip-off, and would rather see waiters in tapestry vests than tuxes or t-shirts." By the mid-1990s, the city was home to many diners who wanted just that type of experience.

Soon, Spike and Charlie's father stepped back from the restaurant, while the brothers' influence continued to stretch across the city. In 1996, they opened jr. in Bolton Hill. A few years later, they collaborated on the Atlantic and Hudson Street Bakery in the Can Company in Canton, and in 1999, they took over Joy America Café, the then three-year old restaurant on the top floor of the American Visionary Arts Museum.

The late 1990s were an exciting time for the Gjerdes, but by the early part of the twenty-first century, things were not as sunny. The stressors and challenges associated with running multiple restaurants took their toll. Spike & Charlie's served its last meal in 2004. In a review published not long before it closed, Elizabeth Large wrote that her meal was "more uneven than I remember compared with past dinners," but she said the pizzas were "small works of art" and that some of the dinner was "very, very good." Spike and Charlie's location had a reputation of being a place where restaurants don't succeed. During the 1990s, Spike & Charlie's seemed to have broken the jinx, though, in the years since its closure, that rep has returned.

But both Gjerdes landed on their feet. "I vowed never to do fine dining again," Charlie said. "I'm not cut out for it." But he's still in the business; Charlie, his wife, Lori, and her sister, Carrie Podles, own restaurants all over the city. Though they're diverse in terms of culinary offerings, they share a reputation for being fun, likable spots. Spike is the culinary force behind Foodshed Restaurant Group, which operates Woodberry Kitchen, a 2015 James Beard Award winner, along with several other places, including Artifact Coffee, the coffee shop and bookstore Bird in Hand, Sandlot and A Rake's Progress in Washington, D.C. A few other Foodshed concepts, like

Parts & Labor and Shoo-Fly, have opened and closed in recent years. The brothers' first forays back into the dining scene—Woodberry Kitchen for Spike and Alexander's Tavern for Charlie—opened within a few months of each other in 2007, and they are still thriving today.

Though their restaurant work has taken them in different directions, the Gjerde brothers' relationship is still strong. "I'm very proud that my brother and I created this thing," said Spike. "And really proud of the fact that we were able to slowly divest ourselves over time, as things got difficult, in a way that preserved our friendship and family." In a 2014 *Baltimore* magazine article, the late Nelson Carey observed: "Wisely, I think they both decided they'd rather be loving brothers than business partners."

Though David and Alice Gjerde stepped away from the business of the restaurants, they remained strong supporters of their sons until they died: Alice in 2011 and David two years later. In a 1995 *Baltimore Sun* article, Spike noted that his mother's attitude and awareness heavily influenced his career. In David's obituary, Bill Struever remembered him as "a fun, good-hearted soul," who was "steadfast in his belief in his two sons."

Their parents' support and those years working together laid the groundwork for the brothers' future success. "The stage was set," for both brothers to make their individual marks on the city's restaurant scene, said Spike. "The seed was planted."

33

Wild Mushroom

A FOCUS ON FUNGI
1995–2000

Trendy foods are nothing new in the restaurant industry. In the 1960s, fondue was all the rage. In the 1970s, crèpe shops were popping up all over. And in the 1990s? Mushrooms were the hot new thing. "Nowadays any restaurant worth its salt has a portobello mushroom or two on its menu, if not a shiitake, an enoki and a morel," wrote Elizabeth Large in the *Baltimore Sun* in 1995. Large was reviewing Wild Mushroom, a new Canton restaurant that, as its name suggested, was all about the 'shrooms.

Wild Mushroom opened on South Montford Street in February 1995. The restaurant was helmed by Jennifer Moeller Price, a twenty-something-year-old chef with an impressive résumé; prior to branching out on her own, Moeller Price had worked at M. Gettier in Fells Point and at Piccolo's in Columbia. She co-owned Wild Mushroom with her parents—common fixtures in the restaurant—and her husband, but she was in charge in the kitchen.

Wild Mushroom was groundbreaking for its hyper-focus on one hot ingredient and for its female ownership in a time when restaurant kitchens were largely the domain of men. It was ahead of the game in a few other ways, too. Nowadays, a restaurant opening in Canton wouldn't raise any eyebrows; it's a sought-after neighborhood packed with young professionals who love to dine out. But in 1995, when Moeller Price put down her roots on South Montford, Canton was quite different. The neighborhood was in the early stages of a boom, with some construction projects underway but by no means complete. The revitalization of the Canton Square area

Wild Mushroom opened in historic Canton in 1995. *Courtesy of Eli Pousson from the Baltimore Heritage organization.*

was just beginning: Nacho Mama's had opened a year earlier, in 1994, and Claddagh Pub opened around the same time as Wild Mushroom in 1995. The reopening of the Can Company was still three years in the future.

Though the neighborhood wasn't yet a dining destination, people flocked to the restaurant. "When I started there, the line would go around the block. We never took reservations, and it was always bustling with energy," recalled Jennifer Price, a hostess, waitress and bar manager who worked at the restaurant for about three years, starting in 1995 (and who shares a name with the owner but is not related to her).

The menu, including weekly specials, was written on a chalkboard framing the kitchen, which was visible through a window that was open to the dining room—another way the restaurant was ahead of its time; that look is commonplace today but was not in the mid-1990s.

During Elizabeth Large's first visit, she was wowed by the "woodsy, charcoal-grilled flavor" of the portobello sandwich and praised the "light and airy" ham and mushroom meatloaf, served with brandy cream sauce. Later, a vegetarian version of the "meatloaf" became something of a star

Canton from above. *Courtesy of Elliott Plack.*

attraction for Wild Mushroom. "We had really neat things you'd never think of," said Price. "A lot of the food was a different take on things, like crab dip served with portobello mushrooms." Other memorable dishes included hand-rolled wild mushroom sushi on Saturday nights and wild mushroom lobster ravioli with black truffles. While the menu mainly focused on mushrooms—"you definitely had to like mushrooms" to really enjoy the restaurant, Price said—it also included some nonfungi items.

The vibe, Price said, was more like a New York restaurant than any other place in Baltimore at the time. "It was very different from any place I'd been. Everybody was so eclectic who worked there. We could wear whatever we wanted. It was very free-spirited." The crowd, too, was an interesting mix, with guests of different ages and types and the occasional visit from Baltimore native and filmmaker John Waters.

Wild Mushroom wasn't just known for its earthy dishes, either. The restaurant's bar program developed a following for its selection of Belgian beers and the entertaining and educational style of one bartender: the late Mick Kipp. When Kipp passed away in 2013, he was remembered for his "Whiskey Pirate" persona, his Whiskey Island hot sauces and his prominent role in Baltimore's beer scene. At Wild Mushroom, Kipp "ran the bar, waited tables [and] greeted guests," said Amy Langrehr, the personality behind the food blog Charm City Cook. "He was so charming and so loud. So animated. Everyone loved him." At the time, Langrehr was just learning about Belgian beers; Kipp provided her education. "They had a Belgian beer club," she said. "He'd give tasting notes, like, 'Now, Amy, this one's going to be really tropical, like bananas on the nose but not in the actual beer.' He was such a character, in the best way." The staff learned from Kipp, as well. "Mick was the bar manager when I got there," said Price. "We had so many Belgian ales, which was really unique. They were amazing, and I didn't even know they existed before."

Building on the success of Wild Mushroom, Moeller Price opened two other fungi-focused places on the south side of the city. Wild Mushroom Merchant, which opened on Fleet Street in Fells Point in September 1996, was a carry-out deli and juice bar that sold items like sandwiches and a popular mushroom sushi dish. Port O Bella, a casual spot with only outdoor seating, opened on Boston Street, next to Bay Café, in late 1997. With its harborside location, Port O Bella was planned as a summertime haunt; it opened in late May and closed, by design, in October. Moeller Price anticipated that it would be busy during the warm months, when she anticipated a slowdown at Wild Mushroom. Despite its intense early popularity, Wild Mushroom's reign in Canton did not last long; the restaurant closed quietly in 2000. "It went more 'corporate,' and I think that was its demise," said Price. "[After Port O Bella opened] everybody had uniforms and the dynamic changed. It went from everybody being free-spirited to more corporate."

Since Wild Mushroom's closing, its former space has been home to two successful eateries: Birches, which occupied the space from September 2000 to 2011, was known for its creative dishes cooked on the restaurant's wood-fired grill, and Verde Pizza Napoletana, a popular pizza spot that was opened in 2012, is still thriving today.

Though it was only open for a quick five years, Wild Mushroom had a big impact on Baltimore's restaurant scene. "It was such a different take on things," said Jennifer Price. "Everybody wanted to check it out."

34

Della Notte Ristorante

A LITTLE ITALY GEM
1997–2013

When people talk about Della Notte Ristorante, they usually mention two things: the extensive wine list and the large tree in the dining room. But that doesn't mean that its award-winning food and lavish décor went unnoticed during its sixteen years of business.

With a gateway location at President Street and Eastern Avenue in Little Italy, the circular building was impressive, with its exterior columns and a moon sign that glowed at night. Inside, there were murals of Italian scenes, carved wood columns, faux-white-brick walls, a lounge bar with a baby grand piano and Roman busts from Haussner's in Highlandtown, which Della Notte owner Ted Julio bought at auction after the restaurant closed in 1999. The restaurant was decorated to look like an Italian piazza, said Rita Lymperopoulos, a longtime manager at the restaurant and now a general manager at Ouzo Bay in Harbor East. The distinctive tree—which had a trunk made of bark, artificial limbs and silk leaves—added to the old-world ambiance, and it was more than just a prop. "It became popular for second weddings," she said. "Couples would have a ceremony under the tree and then eat in the dining room."

Lymperopoulos described the restaurant's fare as northern Italian with "a lot of seafood dishes." On the menu, diners could find items like fettuccine with Bolognese, chicken marsala, a grilled veal rib chop with wild mushroom risotto and swordfish with white wine, rosemary and garlic. "At first, it was a family-style restaurant," she said. "It evolved into a more upscale, fine-dining restaurant."

Della Notte exterior. *Courtesy of Ted Julio.*

Della Notte dining room with the tree. *Courtesy of Ted Julio.*

Della Notte dining rooms and bar. *Courtesy of Ted Julio.*

The restaurant was a draw for many people. Actor Gene Hackman stopped by when he was in town, and in his days before he was president, Donald Trump brought his wife, Melania, to the restaurant when the Miss USA pageant was held in Baltimore in 2005. A private dinner was held for the Trumps at the restaurant before the contest at the Hippodrome Theatre. Donald ate roasted chicken, and Melania had fish fillet, according to "Downtown Diane" (Diane Macklin) in *Mid-Atlantic Restaurant Digest*. Other menu items that April night included endive salad, potato gnocchi and creamy custard for dessert. Professional boxer Sugar Ray Leonard and Olympic swimmer Michael Phelps were among the night's guests. Former Baltimore mayor, Tommy D'Alesandro III, who grew up on nearby Albemarle Street, and his wife, Margie, were also frequent guests, along with D'Alesandro's sister, Nancy Pelosi, speaker of the House of Representatives. "A lot of famous people came," Lymperopoulos said. "[Baltimore Orioles owner] Peter Angelos came very often, almost every day." Ted Julio remembers when actors Will Smith and Baltimore native Jada Pinkett Smith came to the restaurant the day after they were married at the Cloisters in Baltimore County on New Year's Eve 1997. They had crab cakes, he said.

Della Notte shot glass. *Courtesy of Suzanne Loudermilk.*

The 1,400-bottle wine list, detailed in a thirty-page booklet, received a lot of attention. A 2009 *Baltimore* magazine restaurant review said it was "reputed to be the largest in Maryland." Jim Glick, a former bartender at Della Notte, agreed: "It was a beautiful wine list. Ted was an enthusiast."

When Della Notte opened in 1997, in the spot that had been DiVivo's Pastries & Café, the area adjacent to Little Italy, which is now called Harbor East, was mostly barren. But as high-rise buildings, restaurants, and shops transformed the neighborhood into a mini Manhattan, competition for diners increased. "We tried to keep up, but there were too many choices there," said Julio. Della Notte closed in 2013.

The once-landmark restaurant, which sat 230 patrons, was eventually razed to make way for a luxury-apartment tower, but Julio kept many of the plaques that showcased the awards the restaurant had garnered over the years, including a AAA Three Diamond Award, Mobile Travel Guide Award, Wine Spectator Magazine Award of Excellence, Wine Enthusiast Magazine Award of Unique Distinction and a DiRoNa Award. Julio carefully stores them in his Mediterranean-style home in Timonium, where the Roman busts, which were once in his restaurant, greet visitors in the entrance hallway, dining room and other places.

In its review, *Baltimore* magazine called Della Notte "enchanting," adding that the "substantial menu [did] not disappoint either." Glick said he learned a lot from the chefs. "The guys in the kitchen cooked together like a ballet team," he said. "It was beautiful to watch. The kitchen was the most serene place in the restaurant," and the diners were the beneficiaries.

35

The Chameleon

A LOCAVORE PIONEER
2001–2012

Jefferey J. Smith, who grew up in Parkville, always knew he would own a restaurant. He studied culinary arts at the former Baltimore International College and worked at local restaurants, including Martick's Restaurant Francais and Citronelle, before heading to Louisiana to work at Emeril's New Orleans restaurant. A short time later, he was on the road again, heading to Alaska for a job, when he and his wife, Brenda Wolf Smith, experienced car trouble in Montana, derailing their trip. They flipped a quarter to determine their next move—and Baltimore won. They only expected to stay in Baltimore for a short while. They didn't know they would soon be opening the Chameleon, a forerunner of the city's farm-to-table movement, which paved the way for a Lauraville-Hamilton food renaissance.

After helping a friend open Dragon's Breath Burritos in the now Big Bad Wolf House of Barbecue location in Hamilton, Smith was approached by James Hinke, the owner of Hinke's Herring Run Café, who wanted to sell his business. "It was a big break," Smith said. "We did it."

In the beginning, Smith and Wolf Smith called the restaurant Chameleon Café and opened early to serve coffee. The name, Chameleon, reflected the owners' natures. "We're both very fickle people," Smith said. "We weren't sure what to do. It gave us flexibility." The owners eventually focused on dinner service, changing the restaurant's name to the Chameleon and updating its décor from the previous tangerine walls and periwinkle trim. The *Baltimore Sun*'s restaurant critic Richard Gorelick described the change in a 2011 review: "It's a much better space now, more soothing, more elegant, a more appropriate canvas for the sophisticated yet humble, beautifully but simply presented and thoroughly delicious food prepared by Jeff Smith's kitchen."

For eleven years, the Chameleon drew diners to the northeast city neighborhood for Smith's New American cuisine that was influenced by French techniques. Wolf Smith ran the front of the house, performing myriad duties in the cozy, colorful space that could accommodate sixty diners. "We were busy from the get-go," she said. "We wanted people to feel like they were at our house and having a party every night." From the beginning, the restaurant drew praise. The *City Paper* named it a "Best New Restaurant"; *Baltimore* magazine listed it in its "55 Best Restaurants"; and Zagat awarded it a top rating for food, according to the *Baltimore Sun*. The newspaper's restaurant critic at the time, Elizabeth Large, called it a "charmer" in a 2006 review.

Smith and Wolf Smith, who lived in a one-bedroom apartment above the restaurant, were never far away from the bustle. It was "like our dining room," Smith said. "My memories blur home and work," Wolf Smith said. "We celebrated holidays, Thanksgiving, and Easter with family at the restaurant." In the small, open kitchen, during regular hours, Smith concocted dishes like steak Baltimore with corn soufflé, chicken Maryland with lardons and fried bananas and pan-seared rockfish with crab spaetzle. "Jeff put so much of [himself] in that restaurant," said Tina Perry, who worked in Chameleon's kitchen for nine years. "I love it the same way." She remembered when the restaurant introduced charcuterie, including chicken-liver paté—a novel concept in Baltimore at the time—"I was begging people to try it," she said. Perry now owns

The Chameleon's dining room. *Courtesy of Brenda Wolf Smith.*

The Chameleon's frog legs. *Courtesy of Brenda Wolf Smith.*

nearby Red Canoe Café with another Chameleon staff member, Josie Rhodes, who worked as a hostess and manager at Chameleon.

"We had an eclectic group of diners," Rhodes said. "People were really into the food." The restaurant was a community hub, with changing art exhibits, and it served as an employment resource for locals. Rhodes remembered a neighborhood teenager who ironed the restaurant's handmade mint-green tablecloths for several years until she left to become a baker.

After a while, however, the owners began rethinking their lives. Wolf Smith was teaching at the Waldorf School of Baltimore, where the couple's two children, Gertie and Fern, would soon attend school. Smith worried about losing touch with the children because of his seventy-hour-a-week work schedule. "I didn't get to see them," he said. "I wanted to be part of their lives." During the Chameleon's last days, Smith started a business, Maryland Farm to Table Produce, where he matched farmers' products with chefs' needs through a computer program and then delivered the goods. "It was working nicely," he said. "It was breaking even." After a year, Smith realized he needed to expand, which required buying a new truck and a financial re-investment. At the same time, a teaching opportunity for a culinary arts instructor became available at Sollers Point Technical High School in Dundalk. He applied and was hired. "I had been in a stressful job for twelve years. I thought it would be easier," he said with a laugh.

After having two children and working many long hours, Smith and Wolf Smith decided to close the restaurant in 2012. "We burned ourselves out," Wolf Smith said. "We wanted to choose when we closed." They ended on a high note: Smith was named chef of the year by the Restaurant Association of Maryland the day before the Chameleon was taken over by new owners. It is now called Maggie's Farm. Despite the closure of the Chameleon, the couple has certainly left a mark on Baltimore. Smith was named Maryland ProStart Culinary Arts Teacher of the Year in 2017 by the Restaurant Association of Maryland.

Smith said he may consider owning a restaurant when his daughters are in high school. Whatever he does, his Chameleon employees won't forget him anytime soon. "Jeff took a chance on me. He took me right out of culinary school," said Perry of Red Canoe. "Jeff is still the voice in my head. He is my mentor."

Index

A

Angelos, Peter 56

B

Baltimore Colts 81, 112
Bernie Lee's Penn Hotel 108
Bill Struever 153, 157
Booke, Ilene 55
Booke, Louis 53
Boston, Brian 76
Boyd, Bobby 112, 115
Brass Elephant 119, 140, 145
Brooks, John C. 53
Burke's Restaurant 66

C

Café des Artistes 153
Chameleon, the 168

**Chesapeake Restaurant 61, 154
City College 47, 92, 115
Claiborne, Craig 54
Commission for Historic and
      Architectural Preservation 73
Connolly's Seafood House 19
Corey, Mary 151, 154
Crease, the 116

D

D'Alsandro, Thomas 81
Danny's 104, 154
Della Notte Ristorante 164
Dorsey, John 38, 41, 48, 52, 54, 81,
      93, 146

E

Eager House, the 88

G

Gampy's 128
Gettier, Michael 78
Gjerde, Charlie 153, 154, 155, 156, 157
Gjerde, Spike 144, 153
Gohring, Josef 76, 79
Golden Arm 112, 113, 114, 115
Gorelick, Richard 54, 137

H

Harborplace 41, 83, 137
Harvey House 96
Harvey's at Green Spring Station 132
Haussner's 57, 154
Hersh's Orchard Inn 123
Hiaasen, Rob 56
Hicks, Helena 70
Horn & Horn 24
Hutzler's 39

J

Jeannier's 145, 146, 147, 148
Jimmy Wu's New China Inn 92

K

Kaplan, Gail Shavitz 99, 149, 151, 152
Kaplan, Lenny 99, 100, 102, 149, 151
Kelly, Jacques 31, 32, 41, 44, 55, 72

L

Lake, Peerce 78
Large, Elizabeth 55, 78, 82, 83, 93, 94, 100, 101, 146, 148, 152, 156, 158, 159
Levine, Charles 99
Little Italy 17, 80, 81, 82, 83, 84
Louie's Bookstore Café 48, 137

M

Maison Marconi 52, 53, 54, 55, 56, 154
Martick, Morris 47, 49
Martick's Restaurant Francaise 47, 48, 49, 50, 51, 137, 140, 146
Maushard, Mary 82
Mencken, H.L. 52
Miller Bros. 34
Morris, Linda Lowe 146

N

New China Inn 94, 95
Nugent, Tom 41

O

Obrycki's Crab House 85
Olesker, Michael 102

P

Pachino, Hersh 100
Patisserie Poupon 153
Peerce's Plantation 74, 78
Pelosi, Nancy 81
Pimlico Hotel 99, 100, 102, 149, 151, 152
Polo Grill 102, 149, 150, 151, 152

R

Rasmussen, Frederick 43, 114, 148
Read's Drug Store 69, 71, 72
Rehert, Isaac 30
Rodricks, Dan 48
Rork, Michael 78
Rottenburg, Laura 55
Rouse, Jimmy 48, 49, 137, 140, 144

S

Sandler, Gilbert 44, 92
Schaefer, William Donald 40, 82
Schoettler, Carl 54
segregation 37, 70
Shavitz, Leon 99, 149, 151, 152
Shields, John 30, 32, 39, 41, 50, 74, 77
Southern Hotel, The 43
Spike & Charlie's 153, 154, 155, 156
Szechuan Gourmet 95

T

Thompson, George 15, 17
Thompson, Margaret M. 17
Thompson's Sea Girt House 15, 18
Tio Pepe 154

U

Unitas, Johnny 112, 113

V

Velleggia, Frank, Sr. 80, 81, 82, 84
Velleggia's 80, 81, 82, 83, 84

W

Wild Mushroom 158, 159, 162, 163
Williams, Lynn 32, 54, 55, 137, 143, 146, 150, 151
Wiscott, Edward C. 36
Women's Industrial Exchange 28
Wu, Jimmy 92, 93, 94, 95

About the Authors

Suzanne Loudermilk is a freelance writer who previously worked as a reporter and restaurant reviewer for the *Baltimore Sun* and as the food and travel editor of *Baltimore* magazine. She has been writing about restaurants for the past twenty years. She is also an adjunct professor at Towson University in Maryland and teaches writing and editing in the mass communication department.

Kit Waskom Pollard is a freelance writer and research analyst who has written about food and restaurants for numerous local publications, including the *Baltimore Sun, Baltimore* magazine and *Baltimore's Child*. She writes restaurant reviews and an events column for the website *Baltimore Fishbowl*.